the steak book

THE
steak
BOOK

by
Arthur Hawkins

GRAMERCY PUBLISHING COMPANY • NEW YORK

to Nancy

517K0200X
Library of Congress Catalog Card Number 66-17429
Copyright © MCMLXVI by Arthur Hawkins
Printed in the United States of America

This edition published by Gramercy Publishing Company,
a division of Crown Publishers, Inc.,
by arrangement with Doubleday & Company, Inc.
a b c d e f g h

If this is a successful and useful book, it is because of the help I received from a number of willing and informed people.

My wife, a very good cook, helped me evaluate and test recipes.

Emil Buscher, head butcher of the Northern Valley Co-op in Leonia, New Jersey, assisted me with the identification and relative cost of steak cuts.

Clara Claasen, cookbook editor of Doubleday, believed in the book from the start, fought to get it accepted, and worried it through to publication.

Reba Staggs and Monte Fleet, directors of the home economics and merchandising departments, respectively, of the National Live Stock and Meat Board, inspected the manuscript and drawings and offered me valuable technical help.

To all of these people I am most grateful.

Contents

Illustrations

the steak book

"A Nice Thick Juicy Steak"

*T*his book is written for Americans—not that I mind in the least if Brazilians or Englishmen or Frenchmen or Afghans find it interesting or profitable. It is written for Americans because to them—certainly to the men (and to the women, too!)—the last word in eating is "a nice thick juicy steak!"

Steak is nutritious. It is a rich source of high quality protein. It supplies health-guarding Vitamin B (thiamin, riboflavin, niacin) and minerals (phosphorus, potassium, magnesium, sodium calcium, iron) in essential quantities. Both the protein and fat are of great energy value.

Steak presents a mouth-watering picture, and its aroma and flavor whet the appetite, set the gastric juices flowing, and produce a fine, satisfied feeling of well-being at the end of a meal.

Steak is what Mother serves her son just home from college, and it's what the condemned man demands for his last meal. It's what the businessman orders in celebration of having just completed a successful deal and what anyone serves to a very special guest, or a very special friend.

If all this does not seem surprising, remember that not many years ago the chicken ruled America. Political slogans called for "a chicken in every pot!" (not "a steak in every skillet!"). Every Sunday, that special day of the

round steak

cut from leg

large and lean, small bone

top round of high quality is tender

1-inch cut weighs about 2 pounds

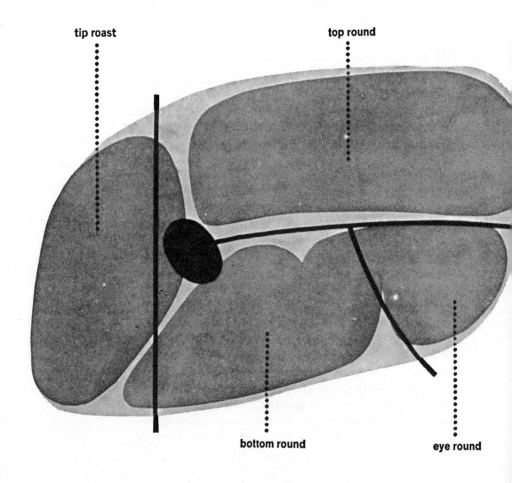

tip roast

top round

bottom round

eye round

week, Americans sat down to the luxury of *a chicken dinner!* During the week ladies out on the town at lunchtime showed their sophistication by ordering chicken salad, and served chicken à la king at their bridge parties. Gentlemen attending banquets or business dinners took it for granted that the menu would include nothing less than chicken.

But times changed. Advertisements for books on etiquette chided the young lady with so little culture that "again she ordered chicken salad." The once elegant banquet course has become "banquet buzzard," a coast-to-coast gastronomic joke. Nowadays chicken must be given unusual gourmet treatment in its preparation to tease the palates of discriminating eaters.

Not so with steak! It really takes a little doing to ruin a good piece of steer meat. But why make it difficult when with just a little effort you can make it absolutely impossible!

So follow along and see how easy it is to become the best steak chef in your block.

17

sirloin steak

cut from sirloin

varying amount of bone

tender and succulent

1-inch cut weighs 1½-2½ pounds

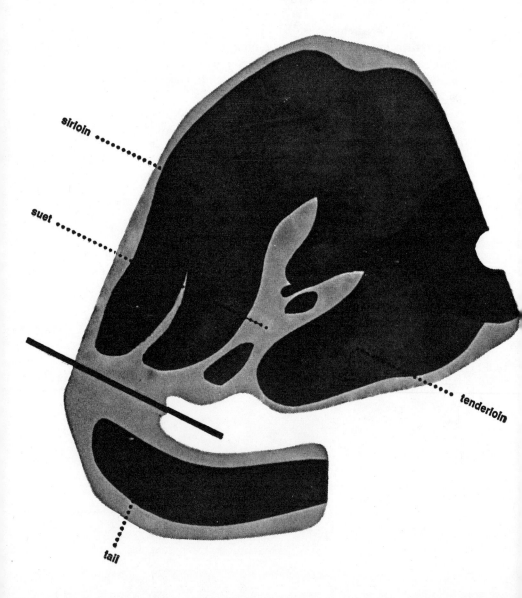

sirloin

suet

tenderloin

tail

How to Buy
a Good Steak

To buy a good steak it is first necessary not to care how much it costs. Steak is not cheap. A thousand-pound steer yields less than a hundred pounds of good, tender broiling steaks. These come from the meat along the back of the animal between the rump and the neck, and consist mostly of those less fibrous muscles that are put to a minimum of use. Equally flavorful but less tender cuts are taken from parts of the rump and neck, too. These steaks, less expensive but with no less food value, are somewhat less tender and require a little more time and effort in the cooking to make them enjoyable.

So get the most for your money. Learn to recognize a good steak when you see it, buy the cut most suitable for the occasion, cook it with loving care, and serve it with the decorum it deserves.

The best steak comes from a steer that has led a happy, lazy life, and met a happy death. It has been well bred, well fed, well butchered, and sometimes well aged.

There is no way that you and I can tell how old the steer was when it was butchered, or who its father and mother were, or how it was fed, but there are a few simple guides you can follow in buying the best quality for the money.

porterhouse steak

cut from short loin nearest sirloin

moderate amount of bone

very tender and succulent

1-inch cut weighs 1-2 pounds

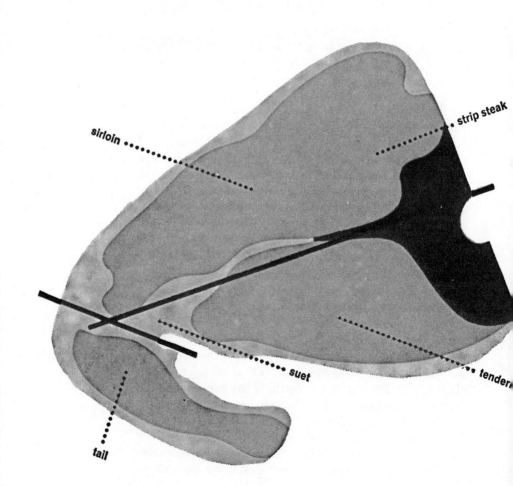

sirloin

strip steak

suet

tender

tail

Look for the Inspection Stamp

a round seal printed in a harmless, purple vegetable coloring indicating that the meat has passed federal inspection. Since 1906 the Federal Meat Inspection Act has required all packing plants slaughtering meat intended for shipment outside the state to operate under federal inspection. This amounts to about 80% of all meat sold commercially. Meat not intended for interstate shipment is usually required to pass state or city inspection but may carry its own inspection stamp. Thus, in one way or another, in these times you are assured of getting a cut of wholesome meat.

Look for the Grade Stamp

which runs the length of the carcass repeating over and over the quality of the meat. Much of the meat sold in this country is government graded in this way. The remainder is graded by the packers or retailers and marked with their own grade or brand names which usually parallel the government names.

The top quality beef is graded *USDA Prime.* (The USDA stands for United States Department of Agriculture.) A steer thus marked has been bred from the best stock, has been more carefully grazed, better fed. Very limited in supply (less than 4% of all beef graded is "prime") and commanding top prices, these steaks are bought up as fast as they are produced by the top restaurants, hotels, and specialty markets. They are not usually available in quantity to the consumer in uncooked form.

21

USDA Choice, tender and flavorful and only slightly lower in quality, is readily found in good retail markets. It constitutes about 70% of all graded beef.

About 20% of graded beef is marked *USDA Good.* An acceptable grade of beef, but with only a moderate amount of marbling, it is sold to discriminating steak eaters throughout the country.

USDA Standard beef, less tender and less tasty, constitutes about 3% of the market.

USDA Commercial, USDA Utility, USDA Cutter, and *USDA Canner,* grades that make up the balance of the market, are rarely sold in retail stores.

T-bone steak

cut from center of short loin

moderate amount of bone

very tender and succulent

1-inch cut weighs about 1 pound

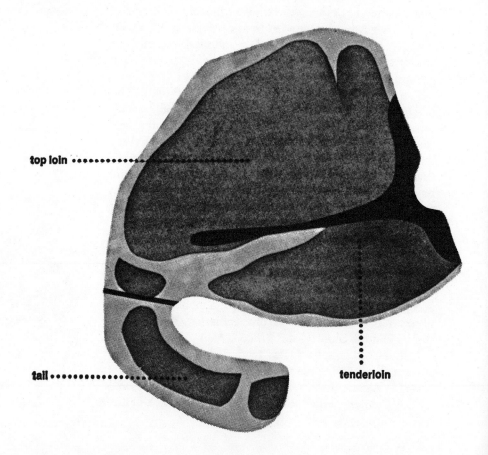

top loin

tail

tenderloin

Look at the meat, itself

It should be firm and of fine-grained texture, bright in color, moist, and free of odor. It should be well marbled with thin lines of fat throughout the meat and coated with fat. The fat itself should be creamy white (the whiter the better) and firm, and the suet should be dry and crumbly.

Learn to recognize steak cuts

Steers, after fattening and slaughtering, are dressed according to certain standard procedures. The style varies from country to country, but almost everywhere in the United States the "Chicago Style" of butchering is followed.

First the steer is cut lengthwise into halves or "sides" (and then sometimes crosswise into "hindquarters" and "forequarters"). The halves are in turn divided into eight "primal cuts": leg (or round), loin, short loin, rib, shoulder (or chuck), shank, plate, and flank (see front endpaper chart). These are wholesaled to your meat retailer who carries on from there. Of the eight primal cuts, he takes steaks from all but the shank and plate. The juiciest and tenderest come from only three: sirloin, short loin, and rib.

Standard terminology for these steaks is as follows: round steaks, sirloin steaks, porterhouse steaks, T-bone steaks, club steaks, rib steaks, Delmonico steaks, chuck steaks, flank steaks, and filets mignons. (The filet mignon is simply a slice taken from the tenderloin, which runs lengthwise through the sirloin and short loin. Since it contains very little fat of its own, the filet slice is often wrapped with a thin slice of fat.)

23

But government regulations have lapsed and an avalanche of new and unfamiliar names has descended upon us, many of them invented on the spot by local butchers to make price comparison difficult or to glamorize less desirable cuts. Steaks have been taken from parts of the steer formerly declared unsuitable for broiling, given a tenderizing treatment and a new name. Or the bone has been removed from standard cuts and a new name added.

To further complicate matters, a single cut can be known by many names, depending upon the part of the country in which you are eating.

club steak

cut from short loin nearest rib

small bone

very tender and succulent

1-inch cut weighs ½-¾ pound

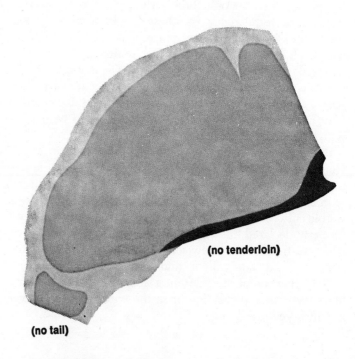

(no tenderloin)

(no tail)

For example, the shell steak, strip steak, key strip, New York cut, Kansas City steak, and hotel steak are substantially the same: porterhouse steaks with tenderloin and tail removed. These steaks can also be bought with bone removed.

Hip steak and rump steak differ very little, if at all, since they both come from the bottom part of the sirloin.

Top sirloin steaks and "Iowa" steaks are boneless cuts from the round near the top part of the sirloin.

Delmonico, Spencer, and country club steaks (and many club steaks) are simply rib steaks with bone and tail removed.

London broil, on the other hand, can come from the flank or it can be a slice of boneless chuck.

Hip bone, long bone, round bone, flat bone, wedge bone, and pin bone are all varieties of the sirloin and are of near equal quality. The last three are the largest steaks the steer produces.

Blade steaks, arm steaks, and shoulder steaks are all cuts from the chuck. High quality beef produces chuck steaks suitable for broiling though of different texture than loin steaks.

Round steaks, top, bottom, and eye, are close neighbors but only the top round of high quality is broilable.

Cubed steaks, minute steaks, sandwich steaks, and chicken steaks are thin cuts, usually mechanically tenderized, taken from almost any part of the steer.

At this point, it might be useful to add a word on French steak cuts. Since the Chicago style of butchering is not observed in France, the process there yields cuts somewhat different from those in this country.

In the first place, the tenderloin (or fillet) which runs the length of the sirloin and short loin is removed in one piece. The entire remaining loin, thus stripped, is then boned and cut into steaks. These cuts, unrecognizable to the average American because they lack an identifying bone, are classified as follows:

Rumpsteak (romsteck)—a part of the round nearest the sirloin—compares to our top sirloin. It must be well aged for broiling.

25

rib steak

cut from rib (slice of standing rib roast)

large rib bone (may be boneless)

tender and tasty

1-inch cut weighs ¾-1¼ pounds

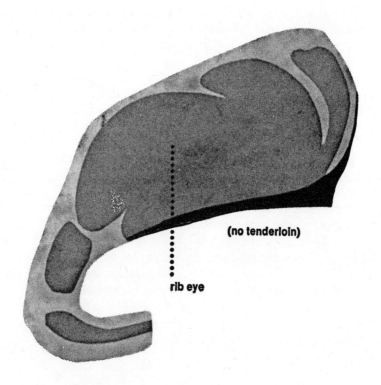

(no tenderloin)

rib eye

Faux filet (contre filet) – a slice of the sirloin. In the United States this is a strip steak.

Entrecôte – from the ribs. Call it a Delmonico or club steak.

Bifteck – a name given to almost any lean boneless steak, but more specifically applies to a cut from the larger (less tender) end of the tenderloin fillet.

Chateaubriand – a two-inch-thick cut of the fillet at the porterhouse section.

Tournedos – from the rib section, corresponds to, and closely resembles, the filet mignon in the American market.

Look at the butcher shop or market

You can usually spot the butcher who takes pride in his product and craftsmanship. The modern supermarket operation doesn't always give today's meat retailer an opportunity to stand behind the counter in his straw hat and greet you in person, but his precut, prepackaged steaks on display do offer you certain advantages. You can examine the amount of bone and fat you are going to get for your money, you can select the size steak you need, and you can compare costs. What's more, if you don't like what you see, you can always ring the service bell and summon the great man himself and order what you want. He will usually be glad to advise you of what to buy for the occasion you have in mind, and will carve the cut you want in just the right thickness.

27

Learn how much steak to buy—and how much to pay

Steak cuts vary greatly depending upon which part of the animal they are taken from. They vary in the degree of tenderness and flavor, in size, and in the amount of bone contained. Some have no bone at all. The bone in steak supplies it with an added flavor, but it is surprising how much it weighs on the scales. Two pounds of Delmonico might serve four hungry people very well because there is no bone, but the same weight of chuck will scarcely serve two.

Steaks vary greatly in size, too, and therefore the number of persons satisfied by steaks of equal thickness will

Delmonico steak

eye of the rib

boneless

tender and tasty

1-inch cut weighs about ¾ pound

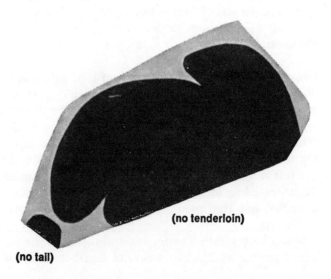

(no tenderloin)

(no tail)

differ as well. Round steak, chuck steak, and most sirloin steaks are large cuts, no matter how thin you slice them. T-bone, club, and rib steaks are smaller. If you wish to feed four with a nice, juicy steak two inches thick, you might find a sirloin too large and a rib steak too small. The solution might be a porterhouse.

All these factors—bone, size, flavor—naturally have a direct bearing on the price tag. So take the time to study your needs carefully. What kind of steak would you like? How thick? How do you intend to cook it? How many must be served? Don't just barge into the meat market and say, "Give me a steak for four!"

The following Buyers' Guide will help you avoid some of the more common mistakes. It might even save you money.

Steak Buyers' Guide

	Bone	Approx. lbs. 1-inch cut	Number Served	Relative Cost (depending upon demand)
round steak	No	2	3	Low
top round steak	No	2	3	Moderate
sirloin steak	Yes	1½–2½	3–4	Moderate
shell or strip steak	No	1	2	High
porterhouse steak	Yes	1–2	2–3	High
T-bone steak	Yes	1	2	High
club steak	No	½–¾	2	High
rib steak	Yes	¾–1¼	1–2	Moderate
Delmonico steak	No	¾	2–3	High
chuck steak	Yes	1½–2½	3–4	Low
flank steak	No	1¾–2½	3–4	Low
filet mignon	No	½	1	High

In calculating the amount of your needs, allow up to three-quarters of a pound of trimmed bone-in steak per adult person, about a half pound of boneless. A boneless steak might be priced higher in the market, but it will serve more eaters and in the long run might be less expensive. Better buy a little extra all around for a cookout.

blade chuck steak

cut from shoulder

irregular bone

tenderest of the chuck

1-inch cut weighs 1½-2½ pounds

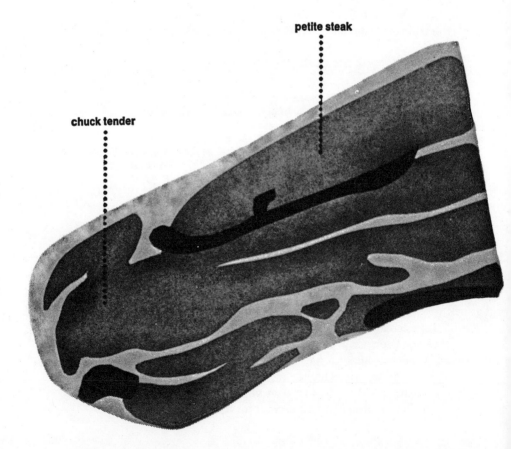

petite steak

chuck tender

Marinating

Marinating is the process of soaking a steak, sometimes overnight, in a seasoned liquid usually containing an acid such as vinegar or lemon juice, to break down the connecting tissues and thus make it more tender.

Some of the grainier, less flavorful steak cuts (round steaks, chuck steaks, blade, arm, and shoulder steaks) will gain in appetite appeal if they are marinated.

The steak is placed in a receptacle just large enough to contain it, the marinating mixture is poured on so that it completely covers it, and the receptacle is closed and placed in the refrigerator usually overnight. The mixture should be stirred from time to time. The steak is then removed and broiled in the usual manner. Some of the marinade may be brushed over the surface as the steak cooks.

There are many marinating mixtures, each imparting a little different flavor, but most of them consist of an oil, with either wine or vinegar or both, and a variety of spices and seasonings. Some contain vegetables.

The following marinades will get you started, after which you can invent your own according to your taste. The quantities of ingredients given are for a steak of 1–3 pounds. Increase quantities for larger steaks.

Marinade #1

Mix together:
½ cup dry white wine
½ cup olive oil (or vegetable oil)
2 tablespoons lemon juice
1 teaspoon salt
1 large onion, grated
1 teaspoon freshly ground pepper

Marinade #2

Mix together:
½ cup dry red wine
½ cup cooking oil
2 tablespoons tarragon vinegar
1 bay leaf
1 onion, sliced fine
1 carrot, sliced fine
1 clove
1 clove garlic, crushed
about 20 peppercorns, crushed
4 sprigs parsley

Marinade #3

Mix together:
½ cup dry red wine
½ cup olive oil
1 tablespoon vinegar
1 carrot, minced
1 onion, minced
1 shallot, chopped
3 sprigs parsley
1 bay leaf
salt and pepper

arm chuck steak

cut from the foreleg

moderate amount of bone

one of the less tender cuts

1-inch cut weighs 1½-2½ pounds

boneless shoulder steak

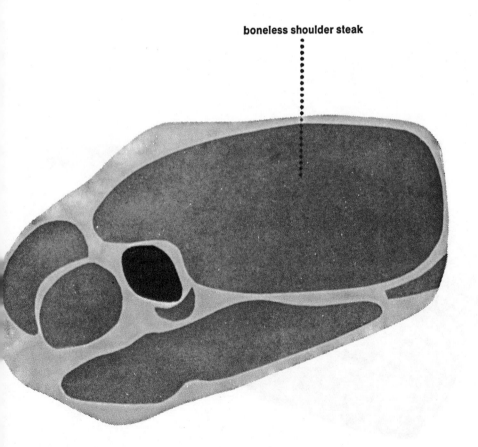

flank steak

cut from underside of steer

boneless

grainy, but flavorful

weighs 1¾-2½ pounds

Marinade #4

Mix together:
½ cup dry red wine
½ cup olive oil
an herb bunch (including parsley, rosemary, thyme,
    a bay leaf)
1 shallot, minced
1 clove garlic, crushed
1 onion, minced

Marinade #5

Mix together:
1 cup French dressing with garlic, and 1 teaspoon
    mixed dried herbs

**tenderloin fillet**

runs length of loin and short loin

boneless

very tender, but dry

whole fillet weighs 5-7 pounds
(measures 4 inches in diameter at its largest)

tenderloin tips

filets-mignons

chateaubriands

tournedos

T-bo

sirloin end

Aged Steaks

merican tastes today generally tend toward mild-flavored steak. For this reason much beef is delivered to the retail markets about three to five days after slaughtering. Some aging takes place in the retail markets, where the average butcher may give the steer up to two weeks at 33° before carving it into steaks. This "hanging" process intensifies the flavor and makes the meat more tender.

Most of the *USDA Prime* and some of the *USDA Choice* sides are "hung" in the packing plants or private installations from two to three weeks before delivery. Correctly carried out, the process is elaborate, involving the use of special equipment to control temperature and humidity. The precise length of time sides or wholesale cuts of varying quality are hung is important.

Aging costs money. The equipment is expensive and the process requires care. The meat shrinks and the surface meat exposed during hanging must be trimmed away. Therefore, in most cases only the meat of top quality is aged.

Since aged steaks with "that steak-house" flavor are so expensive, they are usually to be found only in the more exclusive specialty markets, where they are recognizable by their very dark color.

There are also short-cut methods for tenderizing steak without aging. One uses ultraviolet radiation at room temperature. Another uses a meat-tenderizing enzyme called papain which is injected into the animal shortly before slaughtering. This latter tenderizer is available for home use in the form of a salt which can be sprinkled on the meat before cooking. None of these quick processes improves the flavor of steak, and the papain mixtures can even change the texture of the meat undesirably. Tenderizers are not recommended, but if used, should be done so with care.

If the cut of steak you plan to serve is not tender, try marinating it overnight in one of the mixtures previously mentioned. You will find that the flavor is improved, too. Or try pounding the steak with the dull edge of a heavy knife or the edge of a plate to break down the fibers.

Cooking the Steak

*T*here are only two basic ways to cook meat: by dry heat and by moist heat. Each of these methods has modifications. The dry heat method includes oven broiling, pan broiling, charcoal broiling, and pan frying. Moist heat cooking includes braising, and cooking in liquid.

Steak can be cooked by any of the above methods but should not be cooked in liquid.

The more tender cuts, those from the sirloin, short loin, and ribs, may be cooked by broiling, pan broiling, or grilling. The less tender cuts, those from the rump or chuck, should be pan fried or slow cooked by braising.

Broiling
Broiling is a dry heat method done by direct heat either (a) by gas flame or electric coils in the range oven or portable unit, or (b) over hot coals or charcoal, or (c) in a hot, uncovered skillet on top of the stove. (Broiling on a gridiron is also called grilling.)

Oven broiling
This is a dry heat method done by direct heat in the oven under a gas flame or electric heating unit. Steak for oven broiling should be at least one inch thick. (Thinner cuts

39

will become done inside before the outside is sufficiently browned.) Trim excess fat from edges and slash in several places (not cutting into lean) to prevent curling. Place on broiler pan rack that has been oiled to prevent sticking. Set the oven regulator at 350° and slide in rack two to three inches from heat. Broil until top side is brown (at which time the steak should be about half done). Season top side with salt and pepper, turn and brown on other side, season again, and serve.

Or try the following flame-searing, open-door method of broiling. But you had better turn on the exhaust fan! You will be surprised to see how close you can come to restaurant-broiled steak which has had all the advantages of an 800° broiler.

Preheat oven at maximum heat for ten minutes and slide in rack so that steak is almost touching the flame. Leave the broiler door open (or better still, remove it if possible). This will prevent the formation of moist heat or steam and produce a crisp exterior and a juicy interior. When one side is crisply browned, season with salt and pepper and turn. Brown other side and cook to desired doneness, remove, season, and serve at once on a preheated platter. (For a two-inch-thick steak, lower the rack and cook additionally on each side.)

How long do you cook steak? Who knows. Tastes differ. One man's medium is another's rare.

Broiler sizes and burners vary greatly. Natural gas, artificial gas, mixed gas, bottled gas, and electric burners also vary in the amount of heat produced. To be sure of achieving the doneness you want, try slitting the steak slightly next to the bone and note the color of the meat inside. Or try the timetable below. No cooking schedule can be devised that will be absolutely accurate, but this one will serve as a pretty good guide.

Pan broiling
Pan broiling is a dry heat method similar to oven broiling, except that a heavy skillet is used on top of the range. Steak for pan broiling should be cut one-half to not more than one and one-half inches thick. Trim excess fat from

Timetable for Oven Broiling (at 350° Temperature)

Cut	Thickness (inches)	Weight (pounds)	Rare (minutes)	Medium (minutes)
			Approximate cooking time each side	
top round	1	1½–2	8	10
(high quality)	1½	2–2½	12	15
	2	2½–3	17	20
	1	1½–3	8	10
sirloin steak	1½	2½–4	13	15
	2	3–5	17	20
	1	1½–2	8	10
porterhouse steak	1½	2–3	12	15
	2	2½–3½	16	18
	1	1–1½	6	8
T-bone steak	1½	1½–2	10	12
	2	2–2½	14	16
	1	1–1½	6	8
club steak	1½	1½–2	10	12
	2	2–2½	14	16
	1	½–1	6	8
rib steak	1½	1–2	10	12
	2	2–2½	14	16
	1	½–¾	6	8
Delmonico steak	1½	¾–1	10	12
	2	1–1½	14	16
chuck steak	1	2½–3	9	11
(high quality)	1½	3–4	14	16
	2	4–6	18	20
	1	½–1	3	5
filet mignon	1½	1–1½	5	7
	2	1½–2	8	10

edges and slash in several places to prevent curling. Chuck or top round steak, if of top quality and cut not thicker than three-quarters of an inch, will pan-broil very well. Cube or minute steaks (slices of a less tender cut that have been scored or frenched) will pan-broil if sliced very thin.

Preheat heavy (repeat, *heavy)* skillet. (A piece of white paper in the pan will turn golden brown when it is hot enough.) Place steak in skillet and brown slowly. Do not add water or fat and do not cover. (When a cover is used and a small amount of liquid is added, the steak is *braised.)* Most steak cuts have enough fat to prevent their sticking, but a little salt may be sprinkled into the bottom of the skillet when very lean cuts are pan-broiled.

Brown the steak on both sides. It does not need to be seared unless a heavy crust is desired. Searing does not seal in meat juices.

Excess fat that accumulates should be poured off during the cooking or the steak will *fry.*

Do not overcook. Test doneness by slitting next to the bone and noting color of meat. For pan broiling count on about half the time as required for oven broiling.

Here is an alternate method of pan broiling: Cook steak on one side until nicely browned. Turn and continue cooking until blood appears on top surface. Remove immediately, season with salt and pepper, and serve. This method produces a medium-rare steak.

42

Charcoal broiling or grilling

Any steak from one to two inches thick that can be oven broiled can be cooked outdoors on a charcoal grill. Remember to provide extra-large portions for appetites sharpened by the pleasant aroma of outdoor cooking.

Prepare the steak by trimming off excess fat and slashing fat edges to prevent curling.

Prepare the grill and start the fire far enough in advance so that you will have a good bed of coals at the time you start grilling.

A lining of aluminum foil on the bottom of the fire bowl will make it easier to clean, and a base of gravel about an inch deep will permit the fire to "breathe" and produce more heat.

Use charcoal briquettes and stack them into a pyramid, soak lightly with lighting fluid, let stand a minute, and light. When the surface is covered with gray ash, spread

Timetable for Pan Broiling (Use Heavy Skillet)

Cut	Thickness (inches)	Weight (pounds)	Approximate cooking time each side	
			Rare (minutes)	Medium (minutes)
top round	½	1–1½	3	5
(high quality)	1	1½–2	6	8
	1½	2–2½	9	11
	½	1–2	3	5
sirloin steak	1	1½–3	6	8
	1½	2½–4	8	11
	½	1–1½	3	5
porterhouse steak	1	1½–2	6	8
	1½	2–3	8	11
	½	¾–1	2	4
T-bone	1	1–1½	4	6
	1½	1½–2	8	10
	½	¾–1	2	4
club steak	1	1–1½	4	6
	1½	1½–2	8	10
rib steak	1	½–1	4	5
	1½	1–2	7	9
	1	½–¾	4	6
Delmonico steak	1½	¾–1	7	10
chuck steak	½	1–1½	4	6
(high quality)	1	1½–2½	7	9
	1½	2–4	9	11
filet mignon	1½	1–1½	5	7

the coals evenly and the fire is ready for cooking. This will take about forty-five minutes.

For a faster start (about thirty minutes) punch holes, closely spaced, about one inch from the bottom of a number 10 can, using a pointed beer can opener. Remove bottom of can (top has, of course, already been removed) and place bottom down in the fire bowl. Fill with briquettes, soak with lighting fluid, let stand a minute, and light. When briquettes are covered with gray ash, remove can and spread coals over cooking area. Or, best of all, use an electric plug-in starter.

Start the steak near the coals to produce a good brown crust. Turn and brown the other side. A one-inch-thick steak may be ready to serve at this stage. For thicker cuts, raise the grill and finish cooking more slowly to desired doneness.

For extra smoke flavor, add wood chips such as hickory, oak, apple, or cherry to the briquettes. Soak chips in water an hour or more before using to produce maximum smoke. Add a few chips at a time to the charcoal while cooking.

If flare-ups occur from dripping fat, spray lightly with water, unless a blackened, charred surface is desired.

The cooking time for outdoor grilling depends upon many conditions: the cut of steak, its thickness, the temperature of the meat when cooking began, the equipment used, the degree of heat generated by the coals, even the wind. For all of these reasons it is not possible to devise a reliable timetable.

The following estimates, however, might apply in the case of almost any tender steak cut:

	broiling time—each side	
	rare	medium
1 inch thick	5–7 minutes	7–10 minutes
1½ inches thick	7–10 minutes	10–13 minutes
2 inches thick	10–13 minutes	13–16 minutes

Pan frying

This is a dry heat method similar to pan broiling, except that the steak is cooked in a skillet or fry pan containing a small amount of fat or oil.

Place fry pan over medium-high heat and add about two tablespoons of fat or oil. When bubbling starts, add steak, and brown quickly on both sides. Reduce heat and cook uncovered until desired doneness is attained.

This method is especially suitable for steaks low in natural fat, for less tender cuts, and for thin steaks that have been made tender by pounding, cubing, scoring, or frenching, or when breaded or floured. In general these steaks are cooked "well-done."

Braising

Braising is a moist heat method used for less tender cuts of steak in which a small amount of liquid is added to complete the cooking after the steak has browned in its own fat.

Place the steak in a hot skillet and brown slowly on both sides. If the steak is especially lean, a little fat or oil may have to be added.

Season the browned steak (some recipes call for rolling it in flour), add ¼ to ⅓ cup of liquid, cover tightly to retain steam, and cook slowly until tender. Liquids used in braising steak may be water, tomato juice, meat stock, diluted vinegar, cider, grape juice or wine, cream or sour cream. Acidic liquids such as wines, vinegar, and fruit juices have a tenderizing effect by breaking down connective tissue.

Braising requires more cooking time than broiling, which is why this method is used for the less tender cuts.

Since some of the steak flavor is lost to the liquid in braising, the liquid should be retained and used as gravy. It may be used as is, or thickened with flour and water (or milk or cream or stock), if desired.

Cooking frozen steak

45

Frozen steak can be cooked satisfactorily by defrosting either before cooking or during cooking.

To defrost before cooking allow steak, in its original wrapping, to remain in the refrigerator for about twelve hours. Or you can let it stand at room temperature for two to four hours. Or you can allow faucet water to drip on the wrapped steak (provided no water is allowed to touch the meat itself).

After defrosting, proceed with cooking as though steak had not been frozen.

When cooking steak in the frozen state, it is necessary to allow additional cooking time. Frozen steaks should be oven broiled further from the heat so that inside will be cooked to desired doneness without overcooking the surface. When pan broiling, use a moderately hot skillet so that steak can brown before defrosting, then reduce heat, turning frequently so that steak will cook through.

Steak Recipes

*C*ooking steak is very easy. All you do is supply heat, apply it to the steak, turn the steak at the right time, and then remove it from the fire when it is done. But there are things you can do to steak before, during, and after you cook it that will add variety to your eating.

The recipes on the following pages are intended to provide just such variety—and to stimulate your inventiveness as a chef.

Each recipe begins with a list of the necessary staples and seasonings. There is nothing very unusual about most of these ingredients—they are to be found as a matter of course in any well-stocked kitchen—but before you start cooking, it's best to check and make sure everything needed is at hand. Substitutions sometimes work out satisfactorily and indeed are the very essence of creative cooking, but the end result might be far afield of the original intention.

Of course, you can substitute margarine, but butter is better. Not everyone likes olive oil, and for those that don't, the blander vegetable oil will be preferable. But please don't use ordinary commercial pepper. It can't compare in flavor with whole peppercorns freshly ground or cracked. And never (repeat, *never*) should you expect anything but minimum results from minimum-quality cooking wine. Make no mistake about it, the best wine adds the best flavor.

Some of the ingredients you use will require preparation before using: chopping, mincing, slicing, etc. Your operation will proceed more smoothly if you attend to these things in advance, not as you go along.

The following are supplies you might meet up with in the steak recipes that follow. Most of them are to be found in every well-stocked kitchen.

Staples

A·1 sauce
beef stock
butter
catsup
chili sauce
cream, sour
cream, sweet
flour
meat glaze
mustard, Dijon
mustard, dry
mustard, yellow
oil, corn
oil, olive
oil, vegetable
salt
tomato paste
vinegar
Worcestershire sauce

Herbs & Spices

bay leaf
cayenne
chili powder
chives
garlic
mushrooms, fresh
onions, green
onions, white
parsley, fresh
paprika
pepper, whole black
shallots
thyme

Liquors

cognac
wine, dry red
wine, dry white
sherry

Most of the standard steak cuts can be used for each recipe, depending only upon bone, size, thickness, and degree of tenderness. All of the standard steak cuts have been listed under each recipe, and those most suitable for the recipe under consideration have been starred. In many cases, you are thus given the opportunity of serving a more economical cut or shooting the works.

In every recipe, quantities of all ingredients and of steak are indicated and an estimate is made of how many eaters will normally be accommodated.

As to the matter of estimating cooking time, how do you like your steak anyway, rare, medium, or well-done? And—how rare is "rare"? How medium is "medium"? You'll just have to refer to the cooking timetables, cross your fingers, and trust to your own judgment of your guests' tastes.

Final precautions: In pan broiling use a heavy (repeat *heavy*) skillet or griddle for even distribution of heat. In oven broiling be sure the grill and grill pan are clean and free from grease or the oven will smoke. And finally, steak should be served *hot*. So prepare all the other dishes, pre-warm the carving board or platter and plates. Then cook the steak. Good eating!

Steak Diane

★ 2½ pounds steak, 1 inch thick
6 tablespoons butter
4 tablespoons chopped green onions
2 tablespoons Worcestershire sauce
1 tablespoon dry mustard
salt
freshly ground pepper
4 tablespoons cognac
chopped parsley

If steak contains bone, remove it, trim off excess fat and tail, score edges. Tie up any loose ends with string.

Put steak between sheets of waxed paper and pound until about ½ inch thick.

In a hot, buttered skillet brown quickly on both sides and remove to platter.

In same skillet prepare thick sauce as follows: To butter in small saucepan, add chopped onions, Worcestershire, dry mustard, a little salt and pepper. Simmer slowly until brown.

Return steak to skillet and cook in sauce about 2 minutes on each side or to desired degree of doneness.

Pour on preheated cognac and ignite with a match.

Remove to serving platter, garnish with chopped parsley, season with salt and plenty of pepper, and serve at once.

This entire operation can be carried out very well at the table, using a hot chafing dish.

SERVES FOUR

round	rib
top round	★ Delmonico
★ sirloin	chuck
★ porterhouse	flank
★ T-bone	★ filet mignon
★ club	minute or cube

Porterhouse Steak with Mushrooms

★ 2½ pounds porterhouse steak
¾ pound large mushrooms
1 tablespoon butter
salt
dash nutmeg
2 tablespoons cream
freshly ground pepper

Trim excess fat from steak and pan-broil in a heavy skillet over high heat to desired doneness.

Remove to hot platter.

Peel the mushrooms, select four large caps, and chop the rest.

Sauté mushrooms in the pan juices to which has been added butter, salt, and nutmeg.

Remove the four large caps and place on steak.

To the skillet add cream, simmer for a few seconds, and pour over steak; sprinkle lavishly with pepper.

SERVES FOUR

51

round	rib
top round	Delmonico
sirloin	chuck
★ porterhouse	flank
T-bone	filet mignon
club	minute or cube

Steak au Poivre

★ 2½ pounds steak, 1½ inches thick
3 tablespoons whole black pepper
salt
¼ cup olive oil
¼ cup brandy
½ pint cream
chopped parsley

Coarsely crush peppercorns (put them in towel and crack with bottom of skillet, or use mortar and pestle).

Trim excess fat from steak, score edges, and season with salt on both sides.

Pound crushed pepper into steak until both sides are heavily coated.

Broil on both sides in very hot oiled skillet.

Remove onto heated serving dish and place in warm oven.

Discard all but 1 tablespoon of the oil and drippings, add brandy, and flame for about a minute.

Add cream, stir, and heat.

When sauce thickens, pour over steak and garnish with chopped parsley.

SERVES FOUR

52

round	rib
top round	★ Delmonico
★ sirloin	chuck
★ porterhouse	flank
★ T-bone	★ filet mignon
★ club	minute or cube

Steak Arabian

★ 2 pounds boneless steak, ½ inch thick, sliced into
     1-inch strips
½ cup olive oil
1 large Bermuda onion, sliced
2 green peppers, sliced
1 (2-ounce) can pimientos, chopped
2 cloves garlic, mashed
juice of 1 lemon
salt
freshly ground pepper

Place oil, onion, and peppers into heavy skillet and cook slowly until slightly brown.

Add pimientos and steak slices, and cook 3 minutes.

Add garlic, then lemon juice; stir.

Season with salt and pepper, and cook 3 minutes longer.

SERVES FOUR

53

round	rib
★ top round	Delmonico
sirloin	★ chuck
porterhouse	★ flank
T-bone	★ filet mignon
club	★ minute or cube

Steak à la Deutsch

★ 2½ pounds steak, ½ inch thick
6 tablespoons butter
2 medium onions, chopped
4 large mushrooms, sliced
2 green peppers, thinly sliced
2 tablespoons tomato paste
1 teaspoon meat glaze dissolved in 2 tablespoons
    hot water
2 tablespoons cream
½ cup dry sherry
salt
freshly ground pepper
chopped parsley

Pan-broil the steaks in heavy, buttered skillet over a high heat, and remove to warm platter.

In same skillet add chopped onions, mushrooms, and peppers; sauté for a few minutes.

Add tomato paste, meat glaze solution, cream, sherry, and salt; simmer for several minutes.

54

Pour sauce over steak, sprinkle with pepper and parsley.

SERVES FOUR

round	rib
★ top round	Delmonico
sirloin	chuck
porterhouse	flank
T-bone	★ filet mignon
★ club	★ minute or cube

Steak Loire

★ 2½ pounds boneless steak (4 slices), 1 inch thick
  4 tablespoons butter
  ½ pound mushrooms, sliced
  1 cup chopped chives
  salt
  freshly ground pepper
  2 tablespoons dry sherry
  1 tablespoon brandy
  3 tablespoons cream
  1 teaspoon flour
  1 tablespoon dry mustard
  1 teaspoon lemon juice

In a heavy skillet broil the steak slices in 2 tablespoons butter over high heat (2 minutes on each side should do it); transfer to heated platter.

In the same skillet sauté the mushrooms and chives in 2 tablespoons butter for about 5 minutes, season with salt and pepper, and add dry sherry.

In a small saucepan flame warm brandy and pour it over the mushroom sauce.

Add cream blended with flour, dry mustard, and lemon juice.

Simmer sauce a few minutes and pour over steaks.

SERVES FOUR

55

round	rib
★ top round	★ Delmonico
sirloin	chuck
porterhouse	flank
T-bone	★ filet mignon
★ club	★ minute or cube

Ohio Baked Steak

★ 2½ pounds steak, 1½ inches thick
1 clove garlic, cut
salt
freshly ground pepper
1 large Bermuda onion, sliced
½ lemon, sliced
½ cup tomato soup
2 tablespoons Worcestershire sauce
2 tablespoons melted butter

Remove bone and excess fat from steak and rub both sides with cut garlic, salt, and pepper.

Place in shallow buttered pan and cover with onion and lemon slices.

Pour over all tomato soup, Worcestershire sauce, and melted butter.

Bake in 325° oven for about 30 minutes. Serve from baking dish.

56   SERVES FOUR

round	rib
★ top round	Delmonico
★ sirloin	★ chuck
porterhouse	flank
T-bone	filet mignon
club	minute or cube

Rock Salt Steak

★ **4 pounds steak**
1 clove garlic, cut
1 tablespoon melted butter
freshly ground pepper
4 cups rock salt
¾ cup water

Remove bone and excess fat from steak and tie up with string to retain juices.

Rub both sides with cut garlic, brush with melted butter, and sprinkle generously with freshly ground pepper.

Make a thick paste of rock salt and water.

Place steak in heavy pan and cover with half the paste, making a layer about 1½ inches thick.

Put under broiler close to flame and cook about 20 minutes.

Remove pan, lift off crust of salt, turn steak, and cover with remaining paste.

Broil for another 20 minutes, remove from stove, lift off crust of salt, and remove string.

57

Spoon pan juices on steak and serve.

SERVES SIX

round	rib
top round	Delmonico
★ sirloin	chuck
porterhouse	flank
T-bone	filet mignon
club	minute or cube

Maryland Steak and Oysters

★ 2½ pounds steak, 1½ inches thick
1 pint oysters
3 tablespoons lemon juice
3 tablespoons butter
2 teaspoons salt
½ cup boiling water
chopped parsley

In a heavy skillet broil the steak about 5 minutes on each side.

Drain oysters and heat in a saucepan for a few minutes to start the juices.

Spread the oysters over the steak.

Make a sauce blending the lemon juice, butter, salt, and boiling water.

Pour sauce over the steak and oysters and bake in 375° oven for 15 minutes.

Garnish with chopped parsley and serve immediately.

58

SERVES FOUR

round	★ rib
★ top round	★ Delmonico
★ sirloin	chuck
★ porterhouse	flank
★ T-bone	filet mignon
★ club	minute or cube

Planked Steak

★ 4½ pounds steak, 2½ inches thick
7 tablespoons butter
4 cups duchess potatoes
salt
freshly ground pepper
2 teaspoons chopped parsley
juice of ½ lemon

Season a 1-inch-thick plank of hickory, oak, or pine as follows: soak it overnight in cold water, dry it well, rub it with oil, and place it in a 350° oven for an hour.

Place the steak on broiler rack and slide into preheated 550° oven close to heat; broil 15 minutes on each side and remove to the oven plank.

Brush edges of plank with 4 tablespoons butter and decorate it with a ring of duchess potatoes (mashed potatoes forced through a pastry bag).

Place plank in 400° oven to brown potatoes, taking care not to overcook the steak.

Remove plank, season steak with salt and pepper, and spread with the following maître d'hôtel sauce: cream 3 tablespoons butter with chopped parsley, and lemon juice seasoned with salt and pepper.

59

Garnish with bouquets of buttered cauliflower, sautéed mushrooms, broiled tomatoes, buttered green beans, or other seasonal vegetables.

SERVES EIGHT

round	rib
top round	Delmonico
★ sirloin	chuck
★ porterhouse	flank
T-bone	filet mignon
club	minute or cube

Oven-Broiled Strip Steak

★ 2½ pounds porterhouse steak with tenderloin,
      tail and bone removed
1 clove garlic, cut
salt
freshly ground pepper
1 tablespoon butter
chopped parsley

Set oven regulator for broiling.

Trim excess fat from steak, slash edges of remaining fat, and rub thoroughly with cut side of garlic.

Place on oiled rack of broiler pan about 2 inches from heat.

Broil until top side is deep brown (steak should be about half done at this stage).

Season top side with salt and pepper.

Turn and brown other side (consult broiling table or cut small incision to determine doneness).

60

Remove to heated carving board or platter, place butter beneath, season with salt and pepper, and garnish with parsley.

SERVES FOUR

round	rib
top round	Delmonico
sirloin	chuck
★ porterhouse	flank
T-bone	filet mignon
club	minute or cube

Steak à l'Estragon

★ 1 pound steak, ½ inch thick
3 tablespoons butter
1 tablespoon chopped tarragon leaves
½ cup dry red wine
1 tablespoon flour
salt
freshly ground pepper

In a heavy skillet broil the steaks quickly in 2 tablespoons butter and remove to hot platter.

Simmer 2 teaspoons chopped tarragon for a few minutes in dry red wine.

In a separate saucepan melt 1 tablespoon butter, stir in the flour until brown, and gradually add the wine; stir until creamy, season with salt and pepper, and pour over steak and sprinkle with remaining tarragon leaves.

SERVES TWO

61

round	★ rib
★ top round	★ Delmonico
sirloin	chuck
porterhouse	flank
★ T-bone	★ filet mignon
club	★ minute or cube

Filet Mignon, Horseradish

★ 2 pound filet mignon, cut into 4 equal slices
4 tablespoons finely chopped onion
6 tablespoons butter
1 cup cream
2 egg yolks
4 tablespoons horseradish
1 teaspoon meat glaze dissolved in 2 cups
    hot water
1 tablespoon chopped parsley
salt
freshly ground pepper
4 slices French bread

In a small saucepan fry without browning finely chopped onion, using 2 tablespoons butter.

Add cream, simmer, and strain into another saucepan.

Add egg yolks that have been beaten with a little cream, and horseradish (either freshly ground or bottled horseradish that has been squeezed dry); mix thoroughly, season with salt, and keep hot without boiling until ready for use.

Place filets mignons in towel and flatten to 1 inch thick using flat side of a cleaver, taking care to form into rounds during the process.

Dip the fillets in 4 tablespoons melted butter and sauté quickly in heavy skillet, brush each side with meat glaze, sprinkle with chopped parsley, and season with salt and pepper.

Meanwhile prepare rounds of toasted, buttered French bread the same size as the fillets, and place them on hot platter.

Place filets mignons on top of toast rounds, spoon horseradish sauce over each, and serve.

SERVES FOUR

round	rib
top round	Delmonico
sirloin	chuck
porterhouse	flank
T-bone	★ filet mignon
club	minute or cube

Filets Mignons Flambés

★ 2½ pounds filets mignons, cut into 4
    (½-inch-thick) slices of equal size
1 clove garlic, cut
2 tablespoons butter
4 slices French bread
2 teaspoons brandy
salt
freshly ground pepper
2 tablespoons chopped parsley

Rub all sides and edges of steaks with cut clove of garlic.

Pan-broil the steaks in a heavy skillet over a very high heat until crisp and brown on outside and rare on inside.

Add 1 tablespoon butter.

In a separate pan sauté French bread in 1 tablespoon butter until crisp and brown on both sides.

Remove sautéed bread to hot platter.

Remove steak skillet from stove, pour in warm brandy and put a match to it.

Shake skillet to kill flame and transfer steaks to the platter, placing them on the sautéed bread slices.

Pour pan juices over all, season with salt and pepper, and sprinkle with chopped parsley.

63

SERVES FOUR

round	rib
top round	Delmonico
sirloin	chuck
porterhouse	flank
T-bone	★ filet mignon
club	minute or cube

Filet Mignon Biarritz

★ 3 pounds filet mignon, cut into 8 (½-inch-thick)
   slices of equal size
4 tablespoons chopped shallots
1 clove garlic, minced
3 slices bacon, chopped
2 tablespoons chopped mushrooms
1 teaspoon chopped parsley
1 egg yolk
salt
freshly ground pepper
2 tablespoons butter

In a small pan slowly sauté chopped shallots, minced garlic, and chopped bacon.

Add chopped mushrooms and parsley, and continue cooking.

Pour off excess fat and cool.

Add egg yolk, mix well, and spread over four of the steaks, season with salt and pepper.

Cover the four steaks with the remaining four, place in buttered, preheated skillet, and broil over high heat for 4 minutes on each side.

SERVES FOUR

round	rib
top round	Delmonico
sirloin	chuck
porterhouse	flank
T-bone	★ filet mignon
club	minute or cube

Filets Mignons, Foie Gras

2½ pounds filets mignons, cut into 4
    (½-inch-thick) slices of equal size
1 (1-ounce) can pâté de foie gras
2 tablespoons melted butter
freshly ground pepper
salt
chopped water cress

With a sharp knife cut deep slashes into sides of fillets.

Insert pâté de foie gras into these pockets.

Brush generously with melted butter and sprinkle with a little pepper.

Broil in a heavy skillet at high heat, season with salt, and serve garnished with chopped water cress.

SERVES FOUR

65

round	rib
top round	Delmonico
sirloin	chuck
porterhouse	flank
T-bone	★ filet mignon
club	minute or cube

Flank Steak au Beurre Noir

★ 2 pounds steak
1 clove garlic, cut
1 tablespoon olive oil
salt
freshly ground pepper
2 tablespoons butter

Rub steak on both sides with cut side of garlic, brush with olive oil, and place in hot heavy skillet.

Broil quickly on both sides, season with salt and pepper, and remove to warm serving board.

Brown butter in juices and pour over steak.

Cut in thin diagonal slices.

SERVES FOUR

66

round	rib
top round	Delmonico
sirloin	chuck
porterhouse	★ flank
T-bone	filet mignon
club	minute or cube

Flank Steak de Luxe

★ 2½ pounds steak
1 large onion, chopped
4 tablespoons butter
flour
3 tablespoons vinegar
1 teaspoon dry mustard
1 teaspoon paprika
1 teaspoon thyme
1 teaspoon salt
1 teaspoon pepper
1 teaspoon cayenne
1 cup water

With a sharp knife slice steak diagonally into ¼-inch strips.

In a heavy skillet brown the chopped onion in 2 table-spoons butter.

Dredge the steak slices in flour, add them to the onion butter, and sauté gently until brown.

In a saucepan melt 2 tablespoons butter, stir in 1 table-spoon flour, the vinegar, mustard, paprika, thyme, salt, pepper, and cayenne; add water.

67

Pour sauce over the steak, cover the skillet, and simmer for about ½ hour.

SERVES FOUR

round	rib
top round	Delmonico
sirloin	chuck
porterhouse	★ flank
T-bone	filet mignon
club	minute or cube

London Broil Bourguignon

* ★ 2½ pounds boneless steak
  5 tablespoons butter
  ½ cup Burgundy (or other dry red wine)
  ½ tablespoon paprika
  salt
  freshly ground pepper
  6 slices toasted French bread, cut into strips

Broil steak to desired doneness and cut diagonally into thin slices; place in warm oven.

Make the following sauce: brown the butter slowly in a skillet, add wine and paprika; bubble slowly until sauce is somewhat reduced.

Season steak slices with salt and pepper and add to the sauce for a few minutes.

Place on strips of toast, spoon sauce over all, and serve.

SERVES FOUR

68

★ round	rib
top round	Delmonico
sirloin	chuck
porterhouse	★ flank
T-bone	filet mignon
club	★ minute or cube

Boston Broil with Mushrooms

★ 2½ pounds boneless steak, ½ inch thick,
    sliced into 1-inch strips
½ cup olive oil
1 cup dry white wine
1 bay leaf
freshly ground pepper
5 tablespoons butter
several slices toasted French bread, cut into strips
2 green onions, minced
¼ pound mushrooms, sliced
1 tablespoon Worcestershire sauce
dash lemon juice
salt
pinch nutmeg
chopped parsley

Marinate steak slices for 2 hours in a mixture of olive oil, ½ cup dry white wine, bay leaf, and a little pepper.

Remove steak, drain well, and pan-broil in heavy skillet with 1 tablespoon butter to desired doneness.

Remove to heated platter and place on toast strips. Keep hot.

69

Sauté in the skillet onions and mushrooms, using 4 tablespoons butter. Add ½ cup dry white wine, Worcestershire sauce, lemon juice, salt, and nutmeg.

Simmer for 10 minutes and spoon over the steak slices.

Sprinkle with chopped parsley and serve.

SERVES FOUR

★ round	rib
★ top round	Delmonico
sirloin	★ chuck
porterhouse	★ flank
T-bone	filet mignon
club	★ minute or cube

Steak au Vin, Suisse

★ 2½ pounds steak, 1½ inches thick
  ¼ cup olive oil
  freshly ground pepper
  1 cup dry red wine
  salt

Preheat oven broiler to 550°.

Remove excess fat from steak, score edges, rub both sides with oil, and sprinkle generously with pepper.

Place on rack in broiling pan and broil 10 minutes.

Baste with half the wine.

Broil 10 minutes on other side and baste with rest of wine.

Remove from oven, salt lightly on both sides, and baste again with pan juices.

Remove to preheated platter and serve.

SERVES FOUR

70

round	rib
★ top round	★ Delmonico
★ sirloin	★ chuck
★ porterhouse	flank
★ T-bone	★ filet mignon
★ club	minute or cube

Garlic Swiss Steak

★ 2½ pounds boneless steak, 1½ inches thick
1 cup flour
salt
freshly ground pepper
3 tablespoons butter
1 (12-ounce) can beer
2 tablespoons vinegar
1 teaspoon dry mustard
4 cloves garlic, chopped

Cover steak with flour, salt, and pepper and pound thoroughly with edge of plate. Turn and repeat on other side.

Brown the steak quickly on both sides in a heavy, buttered skillet.

Cover with the beer, vinegar, mustard, and garlic and simmer until tender (about 1 hour).

SERVES FOUR

71

★ round	rib
top round	Delmonico
sirloin	★ chuck
porterhouse	★ flank
T-bone	filet mignon
club	minute or cube

Braised Swiss Steak

★ 2½ pounds boneless steak, 1½ inches thick
1 cup flour
salt
freshly ground pepper
2 tablespoons oil
1 onion, thinly sliced
1 cup liquid (dry red wine, water, or stock)

Cover steak with flour, salt, and pepper and pound thoroughly with edge of plate; turn and repeat on other side.

Brown the steak quickly on both sides in a heavy, oiled skillet. Add the sliced onion and brown along with the steak.

Add the liquid, cover the pan tightly, and simmer until tender (about 1 hour).

SERVES FOUR

72

★ round	rib
top round	Delmonico
sirloin	chuck
porterhouse	★ flank
T-bone	filet mignon
club	minute or cube

Butterfly Steak

- ★ 1½ pounds boneless steak, 1 inch thick
  salt
  ½ cup cognac
  1 teaspoon Worcestershire sauce
  3 tablespoons butter
  1 teaspoon Dijon mustard
  1 bouillon cube
  dash chili sauce

Trim excess fat from steak.

With a sharp knife slice steak almost in half horizontally; open so that it looks like a butterfly with open wings.

Pound lightly to flatten, and sprinkle with salt and a little of the cognac.

Fold together and place on rack close to flame under 350° broiler and broil for 10 minutes on each side.

Remove, place on hot platter, and keep warm.

In a double boiler mix Worcestershire sauce, Dijon mustard, bouillon cube dissolved in ¾ cup water, and chili sauce; stir and cook until bubbling.

Spoon sauce over steak; heat remaining cognac, flame and pour over all.

SERVES TWO

73

round	rib
★ top round	★ Delmonico
sirloin	chuck
porterhouse	flank
T-bone	★ filet mignon
★ club	minute or cube

Pepper Steak

★ 2½ pounds steak, 1 inch thick, cut into
    1-inch strips
2 tablespoons oil
1 medium onion, minced
1 clove garlic, minced
1 teaspoon salt
1 teaspoon freshly ground pepper
2 green peppers, diced
1 teaspoon meat glaze dissolved in 2 tablespoons
    hot water
1 cup drained tomatoes
1 tablespoon cornstarch
2 teaspoons soy sauce
¼ cup water

Place oil, onion, and garlic in a heavy skillet and simmer a few minutes.

Add steak strips, seasoned with salt and pepper.

Add peppers and meat glaze solution, cover, and cook ½ hour.

Add tomatoes and simmer 5 minutes longer.

Combine cornstarch and soy sauce with water and add to steak mixture; cook 5 minutes, stirring constantly.

SERVES FOUR

★ round	rib
★ top round	Delmonico
sirloin	★ chuck
porterhouse	flank
T-bone	filet mignon
club	★ minute or cube

Minute Steaks Bayou

★ 2½ pounds steaks, ½ inch thick
cooking oil
4 potatoes, thinly sliced
water
4 onions, thinly sliced
1 teaspoon salt
1 teaspoon freshly ground pepper
½ teaspoon cayenne
1 teaspoon paprika
2 tablespoons butter

In a heavy skillet fry the steaks quickly on both sides, using a little oil to prevent sticking.

Add the potato slices and just enough water to cover; simmer gently for 15 minutes.

Add the onion slices, salt, pepper, cayenne, and paprika; let cook uncovered until nearly dry and add the butter.

SERVES FOUR

75

round	rib
top round	Delmonico
sirloin	chuck
porterhouse	flank
T-bone	filet mignon
club	★ minute or cube

Minute Steaks Brazilian

★ 2½ pounds steaks, ½ inch thick
2 tablespoons butter
1 tablespoon olive oil
2 tablespoons finely chopped shallots
2 tablespoons finely chopped parsley
2 tablespoons Worcestershire sauce
1 teaspoon salt
½ teaspoon freshly ground pepper
6 tablespoons dry red wine

Place butter and oil in heavy skillet on high heat, add steaks, and sear quickly on both sides; remove to hot platter.

In same skillet add the shallots, parsley, Worcestershire sauce, salt, and pepper; simmer gently for 2 minutes.

Add the wine and bring to a simmer again; pour over steaks and serve at once.

SERVES FOUR

76

round	rib
top round	Delmonico
sirloin	chuck
porterhouse	flank
T-bone	filet mignon
club	★ minute or cube

Minute Steak Hongrois

★ 1 pound steak, ½ inch thick
4 tablespoons butter
½ cup cream
1 teaspoon paprika
juice of ½ lemon
salt
freshly ground pepper
dash cayenne

In a heavy skillet broil the steaks quickly in the butter; remove to hot platter.

In same skillet add cream, paprika, and lemon juice; simmer gently, season with salt, pepper, and cayenne, and spoon over steak.

SERVES TWO

77

round	rib
★ top round	Delmonico
sirloin	chuck
porterhouse	flank
T-bone	★ filet mignon
club	★ minute or cube

Minute Steaks à la Roquefort

★ 2½ pounds steak, ½ inch thick
8 tablespoons Roquefort cheese
4 tablespoons butter
½ teaspoon cayenne
1 teaspoon salt
½ teaspoon freshly ground pepper
2 tablespoons olive oil
2 tablespoons chopped parsley

Make a thick paste of the Roquefort cheese, butter, cayenne, salt, and pepper.

In a heavy skillet quickly broil the steaks in olive oil on one side.

Remove steaks and spread the Roquefort paste on the cooked side.

Return steaks to skillet and broil slowly on other side with skillet covered.

Sprinkle with chopped parsley and serve.

78   SERVES FOUR

round	rib
★ top round	Delmonico
sirloin	chuck
porterhouse	flank
T-bone	filet mignon
club	★ minute or cube

Steak Stroganoff

★ 2½ pounds boneless steak, ¼ inch thick,
    sliced into 1-inch strips
1 teaspoon salt
1 teaspoon freshly ground pepper
1 teaspoon paprika
2 tablespoons butter
1 onion, grated
1 tablespoon flour
1 cup beef stock
1 cup sour cream
1 tablespoon tomato paste
1 teaspoon chopped parsley

Season steak slices with salt, pepper, and paprika, and place in skillet with 1 tablespoon butter and grated onion. Broil gently.

In another skillet melt 1 tablespoon butter; stir in flour and add stock slowly; simmer, stirring constantly. Add sour cream and tomato paste.

Add the steak slices, onions, and pan juices.

Let simmer for about 15 minutes and serve topped with chopped parsley.

79

SERVES FOUR

★ round	rib
★ top round	Delmonico
sirloin	chuck
porterhouse	★ flank
T-bone	★ filet mignon
club	★ minute or cube

Steak à l'Oignon Belle Alliance

★ 2½ pounds steak, 1½ inches thick
3 tablespoons butter
4 tablespoons flour
2 cups water
6 onions, sliced
2 shallots, chopped
1 teaspoon salt
1½ teaspoons freshly ground pepper
chopped parsley

Trim excess fat from steak, score edges, and broil on both sides to desired doneness in heavy skillet.

Meanwhile in another skillet melt butter, add flour, and stir into a thick roux or paste; gradually add water, continuing to stir.

Add the onions, shallots, salt, and pepper; stir and simmer to softness.

Pour sauce over steak and simmer for a few minutes; sprinkle with chopped parsley and serve.

80

SERVES FOUR

round	★ rib
★ top round	★ Delmonico
★ sirloin	★ chuck
★ porterhouse	flank
★ T-bone	filet mignon
★ club	minute or cube

Steak Marchand de Vin

★ 2½ pounds steak, 2 inches thick
2 tablespoons butter
1 tablespoon chopped shallots
1 teaspoon flour
1 teaspoon meat glaze dissolved
    in 2 tablespoons hot water
1 cup dry red wine
1 teaspoon lemon juice
salt
freshly ground pepper
1 tablespoon cream
1 teaspoon chopped parsley

In a small, buttered saucepan sauté the chopped shallots.

Blend in flour and add meat glaze solution, dry red wine, lemon juice, and salt and pepper to taste.

Simmer down to ½ cup, stir in cream, and simmer a few seconds longer.

Trim excess fat from steak, score edges, and pan-broil in a heavy skillet over high heat to desired doneness.

Remove steak with its pan juices onto heated platter, spoon on the sauce, sprinkle with chopped parsley and serve.

81

SERVES FOUR

round	★ rib
top round	★ Delmonico
★ sirloin	chuck
★ porterhouse	flank
★ T-bone	★ filet mignon
club	minute or cube

Steak Bercy

★ 2½ pounds steak, 2 inches thick
  ¼ cup chopped shallots
  1 cup dry white wine
  3 tablespoons butter
  1 teaspoon lemon juice
  2 tablespoons chopped parsley
  salt
  freshly ground pepper

In a small saucepan simmer the chopped shallots and dry white wine until it is reduced to half.

Remove from heat, stir in butter and lemon juice, and strain.

Add chopped parsley and reheat slightly.

Trim excess fat from steak, score edges, and pan-broil in a heavy skillet over high heat to desired doneness.

Remove steak with its pan juices onto a heated platter, pour on the sauce, season with salt and pepper, and serve.

82   SERVES FOUR

round	★ rib
top round	★ Delmonico
★ sirloin	chuck
★ porterhouse	flank
★ T-bone	★ filet mignon
club	minute or cube

Devon Steaks

★ **2 pounds boneless steak, 1 inch thick**
1 clove garlic, cut
½ cup flour
2 teaspoons salt
1 tablespoon paprika
1 medium onion, sliced
1 cup sliced mushrooms
2 tablespoons olive oil
½ cup water
1 cup sour cream
freshly ground pepper

Cut steak into 4 serving pieces and rub sides and edges with cut side of garlic.

Mix flour, salt, and paprika together and pound into steaks.

Brown onion and mushrooms in a heavy skillet, using olive oil.

Add the steaks, browning quickly on both sides.

Add water, cover skillet, and cook over low heat ½ hour or until meat is tender.

Pour sour cream over steaks, simmer 10 minutes, sprinkle with pepper, and serve.

83

SERVES FOUR

★ round	rib
★ top round	Delmonico
sirloin	★ chuck
porterhouse	★ flank
T-bone	filet mignon
club	minute or cube

Missouri Kitchen Barbecue

★ **3 pounds steak, 2 inches thick**
4 tablespoons butter
2 tablespoons dry mustard
2 tablespoons paprika
1 teaspoon salt
1 teaspoon freshly ground pepper
2 tablespoons olive oil
1 tablespoon Worcestershire sauce
chopped parsley

Trim excess fat from steak and wipe dry.

Make a paste of the butter, dry mustard, paprika, salt, and pepper.

Rub both sides and edges of steak with the paste mixture.

Place on rack in broiling pan and broil close to flame for 5 minutes.

Brush surface of steak with mixture of olive oil and Worcestershire sauce. Turn and broil 5 minutes on other side.

Repeat this operation until steak reaches desired doneness (about 25 minutes).

Remove to hot platter, rub in a little more dry mustard, spoon on pan sauce, and garnish with chopped parsley.

SERVES FOUR

84

round	★ rib
top round	★ Delmonico
sirloin	chuck
★ porterhouse	flank
T-bone	filet mignon
★ club	minute or cube

Onion Steak

★ 2½ pounds steak, 1 inch thick
3 cups chopped Bermuda onions
1 cup dry red wine
1 tablespoon olive oil
1 tablespoon butter
1 tablespoon Worcestershire sauce
4 tablespoons beef bouillon
salt
freshly ground pepper

Put steak in shallow pan, cover with chopped onions, dry red wine, and olive oil.

Cover and marinate 8 hours in refrigerator.

Drain meat well and pan-broil in heavy skillet with butter.

Remove to heated platter.

Add to skillet 1 tablespoon Worcestershire sauce, 4 tablespoons of the wine marinade strained, and beef bouillon.

Simmer 2 minutes, pour over steak, and sprinkle with salt and pepper.

85

SERVES FOUR

★ round	rib
★ top round	Delmonico
sirloin	★ chuck
porterhouse	★ flank
T-bone	filet mignon
club	minute or cube

Cube Steaks Coventry Style

★ 8 (¼-pound each) cube steaks
6 tablespoons oil
flour
salt
freshly ground pepper
1 cup chopped onion
2 tablespoons vinegar
1 tablespoon brown sugar
1 cup catsup
4 tablespoons Worcestershire sauce
1 cup cream

Heat oil in heavy skillet.

Dip steaks in flour, season with salt and pepper, put in skillet, and brown on both sides.

Add onion.

Add vinegar, brown sugar, catsup, Worcestershire sauce, and cream.

Cook slowly for 15 minutes and serve.

86

SERVES FOUR

round	rib
★ top round	Delmonico
sirloin	chuck
porterhouse	★ flank
T-bone	filet mignon
club	★ minute or cube

Mignons of Steak, Béarnaise

★ 2 pounds boneless steak, ½ inch thick,
    sliced into 1-inch strips
1½ pounds medium-size fresh mushrooms
2 tablespoons chopped shallots
1 tablespoon chopped parsley
2 tablespoons chopped chives
salt
freshly ground pepper
10 tablespoons butter
4 tablespoons cream
2 cups béarnaise sauce (see index)

Remove stems from (washed) mushrooms and mince.

Add shallots, parsley, and chives; season with salt and pepper and sauté in 2 tablespoons butter.

Add cream and simmer slowly.

In a separate pan sauté mushroom caps in 2 tablespoons butter and put aside for garnish.

In a heavy skillet sauté steak slices over high heat in 6 tablespoons butter about 2 minutes on each side; do not overcook. Season with salt and pepper.

87

Place steak slices on heatproof platter, cover with shallot mixture, place mushroom caps on top, and spoon béarnaise sauce over all.

Place in preheated broiler a few inches from heat, glaze until golden brown, and serve.

SERVES FOUR

round	rib
★ top round	★ Delmonico
sirloin	chuck
porterhouse	flank
T-bone	★ filet mignon
★ club	★ minute or cube

Steak, Butter-Gin Flambé

★ 2½ pounds steak, 1 inch thick
salt
freshly ground pepper
3 tablespoons butter
4 tablespoons gin

Trim excess fat from steak and pan-broil in heavy skillet to desired doneness.

Season with salt and freshly ground pepper and remove to heated platter.

In same pan melt butter, stir well, add gin, and warm gently.

Ignite, pour over steak, and serve while sauce is still blazing.

SERVES FOUR

88

round	rib
top round	★ Delmonico
★ sirloin	chuck
★ porterhouse	flank
T-bone	★ filet mignon
★ club	minute or cube

Charcoal-Broiled Porterhouse Steak

★ **3 pounds porterhouse steak**
1 clove garlic, crushed
salt
freshly ground pepper
1 tablespoon butter

Trim excess fat from steak, slash edges of remaining fat, and spread with crushed garlic.

Place on oiled grill about 3 inches above thick bed of live hot coals (be generous with the charcoal).

Broil about 12 minutes until nicely crusted.

Turn, season cooked side with salt and pepper, and broil to desired doneness.

Remove to heated carving board or platter, seasoned side down, place butter beneath, and sprinkle with salt and pepper.

SERVES FOUR

89

round	rib
top round	Delmonico
sirloin	chuck
★ porterhouse	flank
T-bone	filet mignon
club	minute or cube

Backyard Charcoal-Broiled Steak

★ **5 pounds steak, 2½ inches thick**
1 clove garlic, cut
2 tablespoons butter
salt
freshly ground pepper

Trim excess fat from steak, cut gashes around edges to prevent curling, and blot dry thoroughly with towel.

Rub all surfaces well with cut side of garlic.

Broil for about 3 minutes over white-hot charcoal as close as possible to heat (let it flame).

With a pair of tongs turn and repeat on other side.

Raise grill to height of about 6 inches above coals and continue broiling to desired doneness.

Remove to warm carving board, place butter under steak, and season well with salt and pepper.

SERVES SIX

90

round	rib
top round	Delmonico
★ sirloin	★ chuck
★ porterhouse	flank
T-bone	filet mignon
club	minute or cube

Wood-Smoke Steak

★ 4 pounds steak, 3 inches thick
  salt
  ½ cup olive oil
  2 tablespoons butter
  1 clove garlic, crushed
  juice of ½ lemon
  ½ cup tomato paste
  ½ cup Worcestershire sauce
  freshly ground pepper

Rub both sides of steak generously with salt and dip in oil.

Place directly on white-hot coals (a thick bed of coals of charcoal, oak, or hickory is a must).

Sear each side quickly, turning frequently.

Each time the steak is turned, baste with the following sauce:

In a small saucepan mix together butter, crushed garlic, lemon juice, tomato paste, Worcestershire sauce, and a little pepper; heat until bubbling.

This steak will be charred black on the edges and will have a delicate flavor of wood smoke.

91

SERVES SIX

round	rib
top round	Delmonico
★ sirloin	chuck
★ porterhouse	flank
T-bone	filet mignon
club	minute or cube

Grilled Individual Steaks

★ 6 (½-pound each) steaks, 1 inch thick
olive oil
1 clove garlic, cut
salt
freshly ground pepper
6 pats butter

Rub steaks with oil and cut garlic and grill 3 inches above bed of live hot coals, searing on both sides.

Cook each steak to desired degree of doneness for each individual.

Remove, season with salt and a liberal sprinkling of pepper, and top with a pat of butter.

SERVES SIX

92

round	rib
top round	★ Delmonico
sirloin	chuck
porterhouse	flank
T-bone	filet mignon
★ club	minute or cube

Hawaiian Steak Barbecue

★ 2½ pounds boneless steak, ¼ inch thick,
    cut into strips
2 cloves garlic, finely chopped
1 onion, finely chopped
1 cup soy sauce
½ cup sherry
1 teaspoon sugar
1 teaspoon powdered ginger
1 teaspoon salt

Combine all ingredients and marinate steak slices 1 or 2 hours.

Remove from marinade, place on skewers, and grill over hot bed of charcoal.

SERVES SIX

93

round	rib
★ top round	★ Delmonico
sirloin	chuck
porterhouse	★ flank
T-bone	filet mignon
★ club	★ minute or cube

Chuck-Wagon Steak Sandwiches

8 (½-pound each) cube steaks
½ cup soy sauce
¼ cup water
2 medium onions, chopped
1 clove garlic, crushed
3 tablespoons sugar
5 tablespoons butter
½ cup flour
2 teaspoons salt
½ teaspoon freshly ground pepper
milk
½ pound mushrooms, sliced
½ cup olive oil
16 slices toasted, buttered French bread
8 slices fresh tomatoes

Mix soy sauce, water, onions, garlic, and sugar and marinate steaks about an hour.

In a saucepan melt 4 tablespoons butter, stir in flour, salt, and pepper. Gradually add enough milk to make a thick sauce.

94

Sauté the mushrooms in 1 tablespoon butter and add to the sauce. Keep hot.

Brush steaks with olive oil and grill over hot coals.

Place steaks on toasted bread, cover with tomato slices, spoon over the mushroom sauce and cover with second slice of toast.

SERVES EIGHT

round	rib
top round	Delmonico
sirloin	chuck
porterhouse	flank
T-bone	filet mignon
club	★ minute or cube

Barbecued Steak Sandwiches

★ **6 cube steaks**
4 tablespoons catsup
2 tablespoons vinegar
3 tablespoons water
2 tablespoons butter
2 teaspoons Worcestershire sauce
dash Tabasco sauce
½ teaspoon salt
12 slices buttered French bread

In a skillet combine all ingredients except bread and heat to just under boiling.

Remove from fire and let stand 15 minutes.

Take out steaks and grill quickly 2 inches from hot coals, baste with the sauce.

Turn and grill on other side, basting.

Remove steaks, place on slices of buttered bread, brush again with sauce, cover with second slices of bread, and serve.

95

SERVES SIX

round	rib
top round	Delmonico
sirloin	chuck
porterhouse	flank
T-bone	filet mignon
club	★ minute or cube

Grilled Steaks on Sticks

★ 3½ pounds boneless steak, cut into 1-inch cubes
1 clove garlic, cut
2 tablespoons olive oil
20 small white onions
salt
freshly ground pepper

Rub steak cubes with garlic and brush with olive oil.

Arrange cubes on green wooden sticks (or skewers) alternating each with an onion.

Grill over bed of hot charcoal. Brush, if desired, with your favorite barbecue sauce.

SERVES SIX

96

round	rib
top round	Delmonico
sirloin	chuck
porterhouse	flank
T-bone	filet mignon
club	minute or cube

Grilled Tenderloin Sandwiches

1 whole steak tenderloin
2 cloves garlic, cut
1 cup olive oil
salt
freshly ground pepper
1 loaf French bread
butter

Trim the tenderloin, rub with cut garlic, and oil well.

Place on grill over hot coals and watch carefully. Grill for about 20 minutes, turning often and keeping well oiled.

Remove to heated serving board, season with salt and lots of pepper.

Split a loaf of French bread lengthwise, toast it lightly, and butter both halves.

Slice the steak thinly, place slices along one half of French loaf, season with salt and pepper, and cover with other half.

Slice through the loaf in large sections.

97

SERVES ABOUT TWELVE

round	rib
top round	Delmonico
sirloin	chuck
porterhouse	flank
T-bone	★ filet mignon
club	minute or cube

Montana Ranch Barbecue

500 pounds beef butchered into 25-pound pieces
10 pounds salt

Bone and roll the beef. Salt and wrap pieces in cheesecloth. Dig pit 5 feet deep, 3 feet wide, 20 feet long and build up wood fire until coals are within a foot of ground level.

Level off coals and cover surface with fine, dry sand.

Place beef on sand, cover with sheet metal, and pile dirt over all to hold in heat.

Cook for 12 hours.

SERVES FIFTEEN HUNDRED

98

Chopped Steak

Steak varies in quality and cost almost as much after it has been chopped or ground as before. And the top quality is almost as desirable. In fact, one well-known newspaper cooking editor is said to prefer top quality chopped steak to a porterhouse.

Because almost all chopped steak looks alike, great reliance must be put on your butcher's integrity.

In general, the finest grades come from the round, or perhaps from the tail of sirloin or porterhouse cuts (though the latter tend to fatness). Incidentally, there is nothing wrong with fat chopped steak except that it is apt to cook up to nothing, leaving you a skillet full of grease.

Chopped neck and chopped chuck, if lean, rank next in quality of texture and flavor.

After round, neck, and chuck there ranges a wide variety of chopped beef made by grinding together scrap meat from all parts of the steer. These are variously labeled: ground beef, chopped meat, steerburger, or just plain hamburger. Chances are you will get what you pay for.

Chopped Steak au Poivre

2 pounds chopped steak
3 tablespoons whole black pepper
salt
4 teaspoons butter
dash Tabasco sauce
1 teaspoon Worcestershire sauce
1 teaspoon lemon juice
2 tablespoons brandy
½ cup cream
chopped parsley

Coarsely crush peppercorns (put them in towel and crack with bottom of skillet, or use mortar and pestle).

Form chopped steak into 4 loosely packed cakes and sprinkle both sides with crushed pepper, pressing into the meat.

Broil on both sides in a hot heavy skillet until well browned on outside and pink inside.

Season with salt, remove to warm platter, and keep hot.

Into the skillet put butter, Tabasco sauce, Worcestershire sauce, and lemon juice.

Ignite the brandy and add to the sauce; swish about for a minute, then add cream.

Heat for a minute and pour over chopped steak, sprinkle with parsley, and serve.

SERVES FOUR

Chopped Sirloin Cavalier

2½ pounds sirloin tail, ground
1 medium onion, finely chopped
2 tablespoons butter
½ cup chopped parsley
2 eggs
2 slices trimmed white bread, crumbled
salt
freshly ground pepper

Sauté onion in butter.

Mix meat, parsley, eggs, and bread; season with salt and pepper.

Form into 6 patties and broil on one side.

Turn, cover with the sautéed onion, and broil to desired doneness.

SERVES SIX

101

Chopped Steak de Luxe

1½ pounds chopped steak
1 onion, chopped
1 tablespoon chopped shallots
4 tablespoons butter
dash Worcestershire sauce
dash Tabasco sauce
1 teaspoon dry mustard
2 teaspoons salt
freshly ground pepper
1 egg, lightly beaten
2 tablespoons sour cream

Sauté the onion and shallots in 2 tablespoons butter, add Worcestershire sauce, Tabasco sauce, dry mustard, salt, and a little pepper.

Mix together with the chopped steak and the lightly beaten egg, using your hands, not a fork.

Roll lightly into balls the size of tennis balls and drop onto kitchen table to flatten.

Pan-broil in a heavy skillet with 2 tablespoons butter; remove to heated platter.

Add sour cream to pan juices, simmer a minute or so, and pour over steak patties.

SERVES FOUR

Chopped Steak, Roquefort

1½ pounds chopped steak
2 tablespoons oil
¼ cup Roquefort cheese, crumbled
3 tablespoons butter
1 tablespoon dry mustard or Dijon mustard
few drops Worcestershire sauce
salt
freshly ground pepper

Shape chopped steak into 8 patties and brown quickly on both sides in heavy, oiled skillet.

Combine Roquefort, butter, mustard, Worcestershire sauce, salt, and pepper.

Spread Roquefort paste over patties, cover skillet, and cook 5 minutes longer.

SERVES FOUR

103

Chopped Steak Saint-Germain

1 pound chopped steak
¼ cup bread crumbs
¼ cup milk
2 eggs, lightly beaten
salt
freshly ground pepper
ground nutmeg
2 tablespoons butter
½ cup dry white wine
2 tablespoons chopped parsley
1 medium onion, chopped

Mix together chopped steak, bread crumbs, milk, eggs, salt, freshly ground pepper, and a little nutmeg.

Let mixture stand for 1 hour and form into 4 patties 1-inch thick.

In a heavy, covered skillet sauté the patties on low heat in butter about 10 minutes on each side, and remove them to a hot platter.

104

In the skillet add dry white wine, chopped parsley, and the chopped onion; simmer a few minutes and pour over steak patties.

SERVES FOUR

Everyday Chopped Steak

1½ pounds chopped steak
3 tablespoons grated onion
2 teaspoons salt
freshly ground pepper
1 teaspoon flour
½ cup milk

Combine steak, onion, salt, and pepper and shape into 8 patties.

Heat heavy skillet, add steak patties, broil on both sides, and remove to heated platter.

Add 1 teaspoon flour to skillet, brown, and then stir in ½ cup milk; simmer and pour over steak patties.

SERVES FOUR

105

Steak Tartare #1

**2 pounds lean steak (filet mignon or top round),
   very finely ground
4 slices rye bread
4 tablespoons butter
4 eggs
8 sardines
2 tablespoons capers**

Toast bread slices, trim crusts, and spread with butter.

Arrange ground steak on each slice of toast.

Place 1 raw egg on each serving.

Garnish each with 2 sardines and ½ tablespoon capers,
and serve raw.

SERVES FOUR

106

Steak Tartare #2

2 pounds lean steak (filet mignon or top round),
   very finely ground
4 raw egg yolks
½ cup finely chopped chives
2 tablespoons finely chopped onions
4 teaspoons finely chopped parsley
2 teaspoons paprika
1 teaspoon dry mustard
2 teaspoons Worcestershire sauce
dash cayenne pepper
salt
finely ground pepper
2 tablespoons brandy
4 slices rye bread
2 tablespoons capers
8 anchovy fillets
4 lemon wedges

In a bowl thoroughly mix chopped steak, egg yolks, chives, onions, seasonings, and brandy.

Spread mixture onto bread slices, garnish with capers, anchovies, and lemon wedges. Serve raw.

SERVES FOUR

107

Salisbury Steak

1 pound chopped steak
1 teaspoon salt
freshly ground pepper
½ cup cream
fresh bread crumbs
1 tablespoon oil
½ cup water
2 tablespoons butter

Mix steak with seasonings and cream and form lightly into individual patties.

Coat with crumbs and pan-broil in a heavy, oiled skillet, turning frequently. Remove to heated platter.

To fat in pan add water, season with salt and pepper, bring to boil, scrape, add butter, and pour over steaks.

SERVES TWO

108

Sloppy Joe's Chopped Steak Sandwiches

1½ pounds ground steak
¼ cup chopped onions
½ cup chopped green peppers
2 tablespoons oil
½ cup diced mushrooms
1 medium tomato, peeled and chopped
1 teaspoon paprika
dash Worcestershire sauce
¼ teaspoon cayenne
1 teaspoon salt
4 hamburger rolls

Sauté onions and green peppers in heavy skillet until slightly browned, using 2 tablespoons oil.

Add mushrooms, tomato, paprika, Worcestershire sauce, cayenne, salt, and chopped steak (loose).

Cover and cook over low heat 15 minutes, stirring frequently.

Spoon onto toasted hamburger rolls.

SERVES FOUR

Chopped Steak Barbecue

2 pounds chopped steak
¼ cup catsup
¼ teaspoon Tabasco sauce
¼ teaspoon chili powder
1½ teaspoons salt
freshly ground pepper
¼ cup water
2 medium onions, sliced

Combine catsup, Tabasco sauce, chili powder, salt, and pepper with ¼ cup water.

Add sliced onions and chopped steak and form into 4 loose, round balls.

Drop balls from height of 2 feet into preheated heavy skillet and brown quickly on both sides to form a crust; reduce heat and cook to desired doneness (or form into 4 patties and grill quickly close to hot charcoal heat).

SERVES FOUR

Pan-broiled Chopped Steak Provençal

2 pounds chopped steak
2 slices bacon
salt
2 medium onions, sliced
½ green pepper, sliced
3 tablespoons butter
½ clove garlic, minced
2 tablespoons flour
½ cup dry red wine
¼ cup catsup
dash Tabasco sauce
dash paprika
freshly ground pepper

Form chopped steak into 4 flattened balls and brown quickly on both sides with the bacon in a hot heavy skillet. Season with salt and reduce heat.

Meanwhile, in another pan brown the onions and pepper in butter. Add garlic and stir in flour, then gradually pour in the wine, stirring continually. Add catsup, Tabasco sauce, paprika, and pepper. Stir until creamy. Thin with water if necessary.

111

Pour sauce over chopped steak patties, simmer for a few minutes, and serve from skillet.

SERVES FOUR

Charcoal-Broiled Chopped Steak

4 pounds lean chopped steak
12 large rolls, buttered
salt
freshly ground pepper

Form chopped steak lightly into 12 balls. Flatten to about 1½ inches thick.

Broil 6 patties as close as possible to white-hot charcoal for about 2 minutes, until surface is charred black.

Turn and repeat on other side.

Raise grill to height of about 6 inches above coals and continue broiling to desired doneness.

Season, and serve at once on hot buttered rolls and place remaining patties on grill for second helping.

SERVES SIX

112

Steak Sauces

A nice thick juicy steak broiled just right over a good hot fire and seasoned with salt and pepper is hard to beat.

However, there comes a time when a little variety is called for. This change of pace can, of course, be provided by turning to any of the standard commercial steak sauces or flavored salts, but with just a little extra effort you can whip up a sauce or a steak butter that will impart a new and interesting flavor to any cut of beef.

Most of the following sauces can be made in just a few minutes, but it is strongly urged that you make the sauce before (or while) cooking the steak so that your finished dish can be served up *hot*.

Mustard Sauce

2 tablespoons butter
1 teaspoon dry mustard
1 teaspoon Worcestershire sauce
1 tablespoon Sauce Diable
1 tablespoon heavy cream

In a saucepan melt butter, add mustard, Worcestershire sauce, and Sauce Diable. Stir, add cream, and stir again until consistency of heavy cream.

YIELDS ABOUT ½ CUP

Horseradish Sauce

½ cup grated fresh horseradish (or bottled
    horseradish squeezed dry)
½ cup cream
3 tablespoons butter
½ teaspoon salt
dash freshly ground pepper

In a saucepan simmer all ingredients for 10 minutes.

YIELDS ABOUT 1 CUP

114

Epicurean Sauce

½ cup heavy cream
3 tablespoons mayonnaise
2 tablespoons grated fresh horseradish (or bottled
    horseradish squeezed dry)
½ teaspoon Dijon mustard
½ teaspoon salt
dash cayenne

Beat cream until stiff. Fold in remaining ingredients.

YIELDS ABOUT 1 CUP

Sauce Bercy

1 tablespoon finely chopped shallots
3 tablespoons butter
2 tablespoons flour
1 teaspoon meat glaze dissolved in ½ cup hot water
salt
pepper

Sauté shallots in 1 tablespoon butter 5 minutes. Add flour, stir, and add dissolved glaze gradually. Add remaining butter and season to taste.

YIELDS ABOUT ½ CUP

Brown Sauce

½ slice onion
2 tablespoons butter or bacon fat
3 tablespoons flour
¼ teaspoon salt
¼ teaspoon pepper
1 teaspoon meat glaze dissolved in ½ cup hot water

115

In a saucepan sauté onion in butter until slightly browned; remove onion and discard; add flour, salt and pepper, stir well until brown; add meat glaze solution gradually; bring to boil, then simmer 2 minutes.

YIELDS ABOUT ½ CUP

Brown Mushroom Sauce

To Brown Sauce add 1 cup mushrooms, sliced and cooked in butter.

YIELDS ABOUT 1½ CUPS

Victor Hugo Sauce

½ teaspoon finely chopped shallots
1 tablespoon tarragon vinegar
5 tablespoons butter
2 egg yolks
1 teaspoon lemon juice
1 teaspoon meat glaze dissolved in ½ cup hot water
½ teaspoon grated fresh horseradish (or bottled
     horseradish squeezed dry)

In a saucepan simmer shallots in vinegar 5 minutes; add butter, egg yolks, lemon juice, and meat glaze solution. Simmer until sauce thickens, then add horseradish.

YIELDS ABOUT ½ CUP

Hot Mayonnaise Sauce

1 tablespoon olive oil
2 egg yolks
1 tablespoon vinegar
½ cup hot water
salt
cayenne
1 teaspoon finely chopped parsley

In a saucepan add oil slowly to egg yolks, stirring constantly; pour in vinegar and water slowly; simmer slowly until sauce thickens; season; add parsley.

YIELDS ABOUT 1 CUP

Brown Tomato Sauce

2 tablespoons butter
2 tablespoons flour
1 cup canned tomatoes, chopped and strained
1 teaspoon meat glaze dissolved in ½ cup hot water
salt
pepper

In a saucepan brown the butter, add flour, and gradually pour in strained tomatoes and glaze solution. Simmer and season to taste.

YIELDS ABOUT 1½ CUPS

Tomato and Mushroom Sauce

To Brown Tomato Sauce add ½ cup mushrooms, sliced and cooked in butter.

YIELDS ABOUT 2 CUPS

Bordelaise Sauce

2 tablespoons butter
2 tablespoons minced shallots
½ cup dry red wine
2 teaspoons chopped parsley
2 teaspoons lemon juice
salt
cayenne
1 teaspoon meat glaze dissolved in ½ cup hot water

In a small saucepan melt the butter, add the shallots, and simmer for about a minute. Add wine and simmer down to half. Add the remaining ingredients, season to taste, and simmer a few minutes.

YIELDS ABOUT 1 CUP

117

Cowboy Sauce

¼ pound butter
1 cup water
2 tablespoons vinegar
1 teaspoon dry mustard
1 teaspoon sugar
½ tablespoon Worcestershire sauce
½ tablespoon Tabasco sauce
½ teaspoon salt
½ teaspoon chili powder
½ teaspoon pepper
½ teaspoon paprika
dash cayenne
½ medium onion, finely chopped
¼ clove garlic

Combine all ingredients and simmer 30 minutes.

YIELDS ABOUT ½ CUP

Hollandise Sauce

9 tablespoons butter
2 egg yolks
1 tablespoon lemon juice
¼ teaspoon salt
dash cayenne

In a double boiler over hot (but not boiling) water mix 3 tablespoons butter, the egg yolks, and lemon juice, stirring constantly until mixture becomes thick; add 3 more tablespoons butter, and as mixture thickens again, 3 more tablespoons butter. Remove from fire, season, and beat with spoon until glossy. (If mixture should curdle, add 2 tablespoons boiling water drop by drop and stir vigorously.)

YIELDS ABOUT 1 CUP

118

Bearnaise Sauce

Mix into Hollandaise Sauce 1 teaspoon finely chopped fresh tarragon, 1 teaspoon finely chopped chives, and ½ teaspoon tarragon vinegar.

YIELDS ABOUT 1 CUP

Henrietta Sauce

Mix into Hollandaise Sauce 1 tablespoon tomato paste and ½ teaspoon chopped parsley.

YIELDS ABOUT 1 CUP

Sauce Figaro

Mix into Henrietta Sauce 1 tablespoon Worcestershire Sauce.

YIELDS ABOUT 1 CUP

Mushroom Sauce

2 tablespoons butter
1 tablespoon finely chopped shallots
1 cup thinly sliced fresh mushrooms
1 teaspoon lemon juice
1 teaspoon meat glaze dissolved in ½ cup hot water

In a small saucepan melt the butter, add the shallots and mushrooms, and simmer slowly for 5 minutes. Mix in other ingredients and bring to a boil.

YIELDS ABOUT 1½ CUPS

119

Quick Bearnaise Sauce #1

1 tablespoon tarragon vinegar
½ tablespoon grated onion
2 tablespoons butter
1 cup mayonnaise
1 egg yolk, beaten
2 teaspoons finely chopped fresh tarragon

In a saucepan cook vinegar, onion, and butter for a few minutes. In a double boiler heat the mayonnaise and stir in the vinegar mixture. Add beaten egg yolk and tarragon and beat well.

YIELDS ABOUT 1½ CUPS

Quick Béarnaise Sauce #2

2 tablespoons dry white wine
2 tablespoons tarragon vinegar
2 teaspoons dried tarragon
1 tablespoon finely chopped shallots
3 egg yolks
2 tablespoons lemon juice
½ teaspoon salt
dash cayenne
8 tablespoons melted butter

In a small saucepan simmer dry white wine, tarragon vine-gar, dried tarragon, and chopped shallots. Continue to simmer until liquid has been reduced to 1 tablespoon. Place in an electric blender egg yolks, lemon juice, salt, and cayenne. Blend for a few seconds at high speed, then gradually add melted butter. Add the herb mixture and blend for a few seconds longer.

YIELDS ABOUT 1 CUP

120

Estragon Sauce

½ tablespoon butter
½ tablespoon flour
½ cup dry red wine
2 tablespoons chopped fresh tarragon leaves
salt
pepper

In a small saucepan melt butter, stir in flour, and simmer till lightly browned. Stir in dry red wine and fresh tar-ragon, simmer until creamy, season to taste.

YIELDS ABOUT 1 CUP

Madeira Sauce

2 tablespoons butter
2 tablespoons minced shallots
1 teaspoon meat glaze dissolved in ½ cup hot water
¼ cup Madeira wine

In a small saucepan melt butter, add shallots, and simmer slowly for 5 minutes (do not brown). Add glaze solution and wine. Simmer for 5 minutes.

YIELDS ABOUT ½ CUP

Sauce Marchand de Vin

3 tablespoons butter
3 shallots (or green onions), minced
½ cup dry red wine
1 teaspoon meat glaze dissolved in ½ cup hot water

In a small saucepan melt 2 tablespoons butter, add shallots, then wine, and simmer down to about 2 tablespoons. Add glaze solution, another tablespoon butter, and simmer gently for about 1 minute.

YIELDS ABOUT 1 CUP

121

Barbecue Sauce #1

1 cup catsup
½ cup vinegar
½ cup water
½ cup butter
2 tablespoons Worcestershire sauce
2 teaspoons salt

Combine all ingredients and simmer 10 minutes.

YIELDS ABOUT 2½ CUPS

Barbecue Sauce #2

1 cup catsup
1 cup dry red wine
¼ cup vinegar
½ cup water
2 tablespoons Worcestershire sauce
½ teaspoon salt
2 tablespoons brown sugar
1 teaspoon dry mustard
1 teaspoon chili powder
dash Tabasco sauce
1 onion, grated

Combine all ingredients and simmer 10 minutes.

YIELDS ABOUT 3 CUPS

Barbecue Sauce #3

1 clove garlic, mashed
1 medium onion, finely chopped
¼ cup butter
1 teaspoon brown sugar
1 teaspoon salt
1 teaspoon dry mustard
1 teaspoon paprika
1 teaspoon chili powder
½ teaspoon freshly ground pepper
2 cups water
¼ cup vinegar
1 tablespoon Worcestershire sauce
1 tablespoon horseradish

In a saucepan cook garlic and onion in butter for a few minutes; stir in all the dry ingredients, then add liquids and simmer 20 minutes.

YIELDS ABOUT 3 CUPS

Barbecue Sauce #4

4 tablespoons butter
4 tablespoons vinegar
4 tablespoons chili sauce
4 tablespoons lemon juice
4 tablespoons Worcestershire sauce
1 clove garlic, minced
1 medium onion, chopped
dash cayenne
dash Tabasco sauce
½ teaspoon salt
½ teaspoon freshly ground pepper

In a small saucepan melt butter, mix in other ingredients, and simmer a few minutes.

YIELDS ABOUT 1½ CUPS

Platter Sauce

2 tablespoons butter
1 teaspoon dry mustard
dash Worcestershire sauce
½ teaspoon salt
½ teaspoon paprika

123

When steak has been removed from skillet, pour off most of the remaining fat. Stir in the above ingredients as you heat to bubbling. Pour over steak as it is served.

Beurre Noir Sauce

2 tablespoons butter
1 teaspoon lemon juice
½ teaspoon salt
½ teaspoon freshly ground pepper

When steak has been removed from skillet, pour off most of the remaining fat. Stir in the above ingredients as you heat to bubbling. Pour over steak as it is served.

Skillet Sauce

2 tablespoons butter
1 teaspoon flour
½ cup water
½ teaspoon salt
½ teaspoon freshly ground pepper

When steak has been removed from skillet, pour off most of the remaining fat. Add butter and flour. Stir vigorously, scraping up coagulated steak essence from bottom of skillet. Add water, season, and simmer down. Pour over steak as it is served.

Steak Butters

Steak butters are prepared by adding various herbs and condiments to butter as it is creamed. (To cream butter use an electric mixer or blender, grind it in a bowl with a pestle, or mash it with the back of a wooden spoon) The butter and the flavoring ingredients must be perfectly blended, and the finished product is always kept cool and firm, not refrigerator hard.

125

Spread on steak just after removing from the fire, or just before eating. Steak butters add flavor—accent the natural quality of the meat. There is almost no end to the variety of flavors attainable by using a little imagination and inventiveness. Try preparing a tray of several steak butters for your guests to choose from. The following are easy to make and should stimulate you to invent your own favorites.

Maître d'Hôtel Butter

Cream 8 tablespoons butter. Beat in, drop by drop, 1 table-spoon lemon juice. Then beat in 3 tablespoons minced fresh parsley and season to taste with salt and pepper.

YIELDS ABOUT ½ CUP

Estragon Butter

Follow recipe for Maître d'Hôtel Butter, substituting 3 tablespoons chopped fresh tarragon (or dried tarragon with minced fresh parsley) for the minced parsley.

YIELDS ABOUT ½ CUP

Herb Butter

Follow recipe for Maître d'Hôtel Butter, substituting 3 tablespoons mixed green herbs for the minced parsley.

YIELDS ABOUT ½ CUP

126

Mustard Butter

Cream 8 tablespoons butter with 1½ tablespoons Dijon mustard. Season to taste with salt and pepper.

YIELDS ABOUT ½ CUP

Anchovy Butter

Cream 8 tablespoons butter with 2 tablespoons mashed canned anchovies or 1 tablespoon anchovy paste.

YIELDS ABOUT ½ CUP

Tomato Butter

Cream 8 tablespoons butter with a tablespoon of tomato paste and a little chopped chives.

YIELDS ABOUT ½ CUP

Roquefort (or Blue Cheese) Butter

Cream 8 tablespoons butter with 2 tablespoons Roquefort cheese (or blue cheese).

YIELDS ABOUT ½ CUP

Garlic Butter

Peel 4 cloves of garlic and put through a garlic press (or pound to a smooth paste in a mortar). Cream this garlic paste into 8 tablespoons butter and add 2 tablespoons minced parsley. Season to taste with salt and pepper.

YIELDS ABOUT ½ CUP

Butter Marchand de Vin

Mix ¼ cup dry red wine with 1 tablespoon minced shallots or green onions, 1 teaspoon meat glaze, and a generous dash of freshly ground pepper and simmer down to about a tablespoon; let cool and cream into 8 tablespoons butter with 1 tablespoon minced parsley.

YIELDS ABOUT ½ CUP

127

Butter Bercy

Follow directions for Butter Marchand de Vin, substituting a dry white wine or vermouth for the red wine.

YIELDS ABOUT ½ CUP

Steak
Accompaniments

When you can have a nice thick juicy steak, who needs to fill up on a lot of side dishes?

One vegetable, a fresh, crisp salad bowl, and a basket of heavy-crust Italian or French bread should be just about right for the most fastidious steak eater.

A few of the simpler ways of preparing the simpler steak accompaniments are offered on the following pages. Those who require more elaborate dishes should consult a general cookbook.

Baked Potatoes

Scrub and dry potatoes, oil lightly, and prick skin in several places with fork. Place on a rack in preheated oven of about 425°.

Bake about 45 minutes, until soft when squeezed.

Split open by making a perforated X with a fork. Season with salt and freshly ground pepper and top with a lump of butter and paprika.

Serve with chopped green onions or chives, crumbled crisp bacon, grated sharp cheese, or with one of the following dressings:

Roquefort Sour Cream Dressing

1 cup sour cream
½ cup crumbled Roquefort cheese
salt
freshly ground pepper
paprika

Blend all ingredients well and season to taste with salt and pepper. Heat without boiling.

YIELDS ABOUT 1½ CUPS

Bacon Sour Cream Dressing

1 cup sour cream
1 cup crumbled crisp bacon
dash Tabasco sauce

Blend all ingredients well and heat without boiling.

YIELDS ABOUT 1½ CUPS

Sour Cream and Chives Dressing

    1 cup sour cream
    ½ cup chopped chives
    2 tablespoons finely chopped parsley
    salt
    freshly ground pepper

Blend well and season to taste. Heat without boiling.

YIELDS ABOUT 1½ CUPS

Sour Cream and Onion Dressing

    1 cup sour cream
    2 tablespoons grated onion
    2 tablespoons finely chopped parsley
    pinch thyme
    1 teaspoon paprika
    dash Tabasco sauce
    freshly ground pepper
    salt

Combine all ingredients and heat without boiling; season
to taste.

YIELDS ABOUT 1½ CUPS

131

Baked Chive Potatoes

    6 large baking potatoes
    1 cup sour cream
    2 tablespoons chopped chives

Using an apple corer, hollow out potatoes from each end.

Combine sour cream and chives and stuff into holes in
potatoes. Plug up ends with ½-inch slice of potato removed with corer.

Puncture skin of each potato with prongs of fork. Wrap
tightly with aluminum foil and place on grill over hot coals.
Bake for 1 hour, turning frequently.

SERVES SIX

Baked Dill Potatoes

Follow directions for Baked Chive Potatoes substituting 2 tablespoons dill seeds for chives.

Baked Bacon Potatoes

Follow directions for Baked Chive Potatoes substituting 1 cup crumbled crisp bacon for chives.

Hashed Brown Potatoes #1

4 large potatoes
2 tablespoons butter
2 tablespoons vegetable oil
salt

Put potatoes in their skins into a saucepan, cover with cold water, and bring to a boil. Then simmer for about 30 minutes or until just done.

Remove from water, cool in refrigerator, and remove skins.

Chop into cubes somewhat smaller than sugar lumps.

Fry in skillet in butter and oil over high heat, turning frequently so that all sides become uniformly browned. Sprinkle with salt.

SERVES FOUR

Hashed Brown Potatoes #2

4 cups parboiled potatoes, peeled and finely diced
1 tablespoon chopped onion
¼ cup butter
salt
pepper
1 tablespoon chopped parsley

In a large skillet sauté the onion in the butter.

Season the potatoes with salt and pepper and add to the onion.

Stir with fork and pat down to a flat cake.

Cover skillet and cook until the bottom of cake is brown.

Flip and brown on other side, sprinkle with parsley.

SERVES FOUR

Oven French Fries

4 cups small potatoes, peeled and cut lengthwise into
    eighths
1 tablespoon vegetable oil
½ cup melted butter
salt

Soak potatoes in cold water ½ hour, drain, and dry with paper towel.

Place in a greased shallow baking pan, brush well with melted butter, and bake in 450° oven until lightly browned, turning occasionally. The whole job should take about ½ hour.

Season with salt and serve.

SERVES FOUR

Broiled Tomatoes

6 fresh ripe tomatoes
2 eggs
4 tablespoons milk
cracker meal
4 tablespoons butter
salt
pepper
chopped parsley

133

Cut tops and bottoms from the tomatoes and slice in half horizontally.

Beat together eggs and milk.

Dip tomato halves in this mixture and dredge with cracker meal.

Broil slowly in heavy saucepan in butter until brown on both sides.

Season with salt and pepper and garnish with chopped parsley.

SERVES FOUR

Steamed Corn-on-the-Cob

Remove heavy outer husks, pull back inner husks, remove silk and trim ears if necessary, and replace husks into original position.

In a large, covered skillet simmer ears until tender in just enough water to maintain steam.

Grilled Garlic Corn

fresh corn-on-the-cob
butter
garlic

Remove heavy outer husks, pull back inner husks, remove silk, and trim ears if necessary.

Prepare garlic butter by adding crushed garlic to melted butter.

134

Brush corn ears generously with melted garlic butter.

Replace inner husks into their original position and tie.

Place on grill above hot coals and broil for about 20 minutes, turning frequently.

Bacon-Wrapped Corn-on-the-Cob

fresh corn-on-the-cob
salt
sliced lean bacon

Husk corn and soak in salted water about ½ hour.

Dry corn, sprinkle with salt, and wrap spirally with bacon, 2 slices for each ear, fastening bacon with wet toothpicks.

Grill over hot coals about 15 minutes, turning frequently.

Fresh Mushrooms

Wash mushrooms well and drain immediately—do not let them soak. Peel only if tough or brown. Leave whole, slice lengthwise, or leave caps whole and chop stems.

To broil, brush with olive oil, season with salt and pepper, and broil slowly in a skillet or broiler and serve on steak.

To fry, simmer about 10 minutes in a generous amount of butter and serve on steak.

French Fried Onion Rings

4 large white or yellow onions
2 teaspoons salt
1 cup milk
1 cup flour
2 cups shortening

Peel onions, cut in slices ¼ inch thick, and separate into rings.

Let onion rings stand in salted milk a few minutes, then drop into paper bag containing flour. Shake until onion rings are well coated.

In a heavy saucepan heat shortening until it is almost smoking-hot, drop in onion rings a few at a time, and fry until lightly browned.

Drain on paper towel, sprinkle with salt, and serve on steak.

SERVES FOUR

Salads

*T*he basic salad of classic cooking consists of raw mixed greens tossed with a French dressing of oil and vinegar. The greens may be any of a variety of lettuces (Boston, romaine, chicory, Bibb), endive, water cress, dandelion greens, even spinach and beet tops.

The greens may be mixed in any combinations, or they may be used alone, but it is most important that they be fresh.

To make a good salad, first wash the greens well in cold water.Then shake them out and drain them in a salad basket to remove excess moisture. Next (and this is most important of all) blot them thoroughly, leaf by leaf, with a towel until absolutely dry, or the oil you later mix in will not adhere to the leaves. As the greens are wiped dry they may be broken, if desired, into bite-size pieces by hand (do not cut lettuces with a knife).

When you are ready to serve the salad, put the greens in a salad bowl that has been rubbed with garlic, then pour on the basic French dressing and mix with your hands, or toss with a wooden spoon and fork until each leaf is well coated and no dressing remains in the bottom of the bowl. Season to taste with salt and freshly ground pepper. Chopped herbs (chives, chervil, parsley, tarragon) in any combination may be sprinkled over the salad before tossing.

This basic salad may be garnished with any combination of the following (or with almost anything else you can think of):

radishes
olives (green or ripe)
sliced tomatoes
sliced cucumbers
julienned carrots
celery
raw mushrooms
sliced hard-cooked eggs
sliced onions
green onions
diced cooked beets
crisp bacon
anchovies
julienned ham, chicken, turkey
sliced green peppers
pimientos
croutons fried in bacon or olive oil

138 Basic French Dressing

Mix well 3 parts olive oil with 1 part vinegar (vary proportions of ingredients to make more, or less, sour).

The French dressing may be varied by substituting lemon juice for vinegar or by adding certain staples or condiments:

Creamy French Dressing

To French dressing add mayonnaise.

Indian Dressing

To French dressing add a pinch of curry powder and chopped hard-cooked egg.

Catsup Dressing

To French dressing add tomato catsup, a pinch of dry mustard, and a dash of paprika.

Vinaigrette Dressing

To French dressing add finely chopped onion, mixed herbs, capers, and chopped hard-cooked egg.

Roquefort (Blue Cheese) Dressing

To French dressing add crumbled Roquefort (blue) cheese, cream, and paprika.

Finally, a mayonnaise-base dressing may be used in place of French dressing. Four of the most popular of these are given below:

Green Mayonnaise

To mayonnaise add finely chopped water cress.

Remoulade Dressing

To mayonnaise add chopped hard-cooked egg, chopped capers, chopped chives and mixed chopped parsley, tarragon, and chervil.

139

Russian Dressing

To mayonnaise add chili sauce, chopped onion, chopped green pepper, chopped pimiento, chopped celery; caviar and a little lemon juice may be added if desired.

Thousand Islands Dressing

To mayonnaise add chili sauce, 12 stuffed olives chopped, chopped green pepper, chopped hard-cooked egg, chopped green onions, and heavy cream whipped; season with salt, pepper, and paprika.

What to Drink with Steak

Wines

To complement a fine steak dinner there is nothing better to drink than wine.

Wine stimulates conversation and promotes a warm feeling among guests. It aids in the digestion of the meal and brings out the flavor of the steak to the fullest. And finally, it leaves a warm afterglow when the meal is finished.

Far too much has been written about the ritual of wine—how to serve it, the proper glass to use, which wine to serve with what course. Wine may be properly served and enjoyed in any type of glass, with or without stem.

In selecting a type of wine to serve with steak, the only criterion should be, which wine tastes best—which wine makes the steak taste best.

Most steak eaters and wine drinkers agree that the robust flavor of red meat is best complemented by a robust, flavorful red wine. But there are many in the white wine-growing provinces of Europe who regularly serve white Burgundies, white Chiantis, and other white wines with red meat and love it. And there are others who will pour you a glass of "pink" wine or rosé (a white wine blended with the skin squeezings of red grapes).

If you are in doubt, serve a Burgundy wine from France, the most robust of all wines, or a Beaujolais, or a Bordeaux (claret) such as Saint-Emilion, or Médoc (one of the lighter red wines).

Or serve a red Chianti from Italy.

Or serve the equivalent of one of the above wines grown in California or New York.

Serve the wine simply, but serve it right. Trim the foil from the cork with a knife and wipe the cork with a clean napkin. Insert the point of the corkscrew into dead center, screw in, and pull out. Wipe the rim of the bottle clean. Pour a little wine into your own glass first and taste (it could be sour or there could be bits of cork in the first serving), serve your guests, then finish serving yourself.

Beer and Ale

If you don't like wine, the next best drink to serve with steak is beer or ale. Serve it cold in prechilled glasses.

For a large party, serve draught beer available in most places in ¼ barrels or ½ barrels set up by your dealer ready to draw.

142

Coffee

Everybody has his own brand of coffee and his own method of brewing it and serving it, iced or hot, large cup or demitasse. But because a steak dinner is very special you might like to top it off with a very special coffee.

Try serving the coffee with a choice of toppings: whipped cream, lemon whipped cream (whipped cream into which grated lemon peel has been whipped) or chocolate whipped cream (whip in instant sweetened cocoa or chocolate powder).

Or shoot the works and serve up one of the following glamour coffees:

Café Brûlot

8 lumps sugar
4 whole cloves
1 cinnamon stick
1 lemon peel cut into a spiral
1 orange peel cut into a spiral
½ cup cognac
2 cups very hot extra strong (demitasse) coffee

Place sugar, cloves, and cinnamon in chafing dish or other suitable container.

Add lemon peel and orange peel.

Add cognac, set over flame, and heat, stirring constantly.

Ignite cognac, continuing to stir.

After about 1 minute, slowly pour in the hot coffee, continuing to stir.

Ladle into demitasse cups while still flaming (taking care not to serve the spices or peels) and serve at once.

SERVES FOUR

143

Coffee Carioca

2 tablespoons sugar
1 orange peel, sliced
¼ cup coffee, ground fine
2 cups boiling water
½ cup dark rum
¼ cup sweetened whipped cream

Place in a heatproof bowl sugar, orange peel, and coffee.

Stir in boiling water and let stand ½ hour.

Strain into coffeepot and heat to just under boiling.

Stir in rum, pour into demitasse cups, and serve topped with whipped cream and garnished with a little grated orange peel.

SERVES FOUR

Café Chantilly

To a demitasse of hot coffee add 1 tablespoon cognac. Float a teaspoon of heavy cream on top.

Irish Coffee

In a wineglass place 2 teaspoons sugar, 2 tablespoons of Irish whiskey, and a little strong hot coffee. Stir to dissolve sugar, nicely fill glass with more coffee, and float a teaspoon of heavy cream on top, or top with whipped cream.

Grog

2 tablespoons butter
½ pound brown sugar
pinch cinnamon
pinch nutmeg
pinch allspice
pinch cloves
pinch salt
lemon peel
orange peel
light rum
heavy cream
very hot coffee

Cream the butter with the brown sugar, add the spices, and mix thoroughly. This spice base can be kept under refrigeration indefinitely in a covered container.

In a 6-ounce mug, put 1 teaspoon of spiced mixture and add a strip each of lemon and orange peel.

Add 3 tablespoons light rum and 2 tablespoons heavy cream.

Fill mug with steaming hot coffee.

Café Orléans Flambé

4 tablespoons brown sugar
2 whole allspice
1 cinnamon stick
1 teaspoon grated lemon peel
2 cups hot strong coffee
½ cup cognac

In a chafing dish combine sugar, spices, lemon peel, and coffee. Heat to just below boiling, stirring constantly.

In a warm ladle heat cognac and ignite.

Quickly pour over coffee mixture, stir, and ladle into demi-tasse cups.

SERVES FOUR

Caffe Borgia

In a large demitasse combine hot Italian coffee and hot chocolate in equal quantities. Top with sweetened whipped cream and sprinkle with grated orange peel.

145

Caffe Cappuccino

In a large demitasse combine equal quantities hot Italian coffee and heavy cream. Sprinkle with cinnamon and nutmeg and serve with lump sugar.

Caffe Chocolaccino

Follow recipe for Caffe Cappuccino and top with sweetened whipped cream and chocolate shavings.

Cowboy Chuck-Wagon Coffee

2 eggs
2 cups cold water
dash salt
1 cup coffee
12 cups boiling water

Wash eggs, break, and beat slightly.

Add 1 cup cold water, egg shells, salt and coffee.

Place in large coffeepot and add boiling water. Stir well. Stuff spout with paper to prevent escape of fragrant aroma.

Set over direct heat, bring slowly to a boil, and boil 3 minutes.

Remove from direct heat and pour in 1 cup cold water to clear (cold water, being heavier than hot, sinks to bottom of pot, carrying grounds with it).

Let stand 10 minutes near fire and serve.

SERVES FIFTEEN

146

Carving and Serving Steak

Many home chefs, after cooking steak with love and devotion, fail to carry through when it comes to carving and serving. The proper routine is really very simple, and adds to the full enjoyment of the meal. Here's how you carve a bone-in steak which is to serve more than one person:

Place steak on a prewarmed platter or carving board (a carving board is better because it doesn't dull the edges of the knife).

With a sharp knife cut around all the bone as closely as possible, remove it, and discard it.

Trim away any rough edges or large morsels of fat that might remain.

Slice long, slender strips (1–2 inches wide depending upon thickness) across steak that include both sirloin and tenderloin portions from the bone end to the tail end.

Serve each guest with a variety of these slices with a little juice spooned on.

The same procedure should, of course, be observed for most boneless steak cuts, the slices being reduced in width as the steak increases in thickness.

An exception is made in the case of flank steak which, because it is not very thick and the texture is comparatively coarse, is always sliced very thin and on the diagonal to attain greater width for each slice.

Steak knives, even when the steak is tender, add to eating enjoyment, and because steak cools quickly, dinner plates must be preheated. Do not serve on the same plate food of a runny nature that would mix with or dilute the natural juices or sauce of the steak.

Some Cooking Terms
Steak Chefs Should Know

baste — to moisten with spoons of juice during cooking.

blend — to mix well.

braise — to cook gently in a covered pot with a minimum of liquid.

broil — to dry-cook under open heat or on a rack in broiler.

brush — to moisten during cooking with a kitchen brush dipped in sauce or marinade.

cream (butter) — to work butter in a round-bottomed bowl at room temperature with a pestle or the back of a wooden spoon until creamy.

decant — to pour out, allowing sediment to remain.

deglaze — to make a concentrated essence by scraping coagulated juices from bottom of skillet and simmering with water or other liquid.

flambé — to flavor with flaming brandy.

french — to tenderize a tough cut by cutting the fibers with a sharp knife or using a frenching device employing sharp needles.

fry — to cook in fat.

grill — to broil next to open heat on a rack.

lard — to lace with a lacing (larding) needle threaded with thin strips of pork fat.

marinate — to soak in a mixture of oil, acid (usually vinegar), and spices.

pan-broil — to dry-cook in a heavy skillet or frying pan.

sauté — to cook in fat over moderate heat.

sear — to cook quickly at high heat (can be in oven or on top of range).

simmer — to cook in liquid below boiling.

P.S.

The word steak comes from an old Saxon word, steik. When the Saxons conquered Britain they brought along their skills as cattlemen, their appetites as beef eaters, and their cooking methods of broiling beef cuts on pointed sticks or stakes over the campfire.

Later a British king was credited with honoring his favorite meat by dubbing the steak "Sir Loin."

Porterhouse steak was named for a New York porter and ale house in the early 1800s that accommodated overflow crowds of customers by hurriedly cutting through sirloin roasts to produce steaks.

The club steak was so called because of its convenient size for banquet service.

The cut adjoining received its name from its T-shaped bone.

Delmonico steak was named for the famous New York restaurateur.

Flank steak was once considered unfit for sale as a steak, but the butcher, knowing it to be a delicious, flavorful cut, took it home to eat himself. Flank steak eventually became known as "butcher's tenderloin."

Suggestion: if the butcher sells you a sirloin or porterhouse with a great deal of tail, ask him to grind the tail and tie it back in place against the steak, or wrap it separately to be used as ground sirloin.

Before pan-broiling, wipe the steak dry and it will brown more quickly and more evenly.

Steak will cook more evenly, too, if it is brought to room temperature before cooking.

Cut small gashes into the fat edges (but not into the lean) of steak before broiling and it will not curl.

152

To test the doneness of steak, cut a small slit next to the bone and examine color of inside.

Do not presalt steak if you wish it to retain its juices.

To pan-broil a 1-inch-thick steak medium rare every time, brown it in a preheated skillet for 3 minutes and turn. Remove and serve the moment a little red juice begins to ooze from the cooked surface. The whole operation should take 5–6 minutes.

In pan-broiling steak, don't forget to pour off excess fat as it accumulates, or the steak will be fried.

To deglaze a skillet after pan-broiling a steak, pour off excess fat, heat, and swish with a little water, wine, or stock. Scrape coagulated juices from bottom of skillet, simmer a second, add a dab of butter, and you have a concentrated essence for spooning over the steak.

To thicken the above essence, add a teaspoon of flour to the pan and brown before swishing with the liquid.

In charcoal cookery, when the fat catches fire and flames envelop the steak they may be extinguished with a toy water pistol or other spray.

A convenient tool for handling steak is a pair of tongs. Tongs also prevent the loss of juices caused by the prick of a fork.

A convenient tool for applying a sauce or marinade to a charcoal-broiling steak is an ordinary paintbrush.

In measuring ingredients, "tablespoon," "teaspoon," and "cup" are understood to be level, not heaped.

Brandy flames only when warmed.

INDEX